The Beautiful Game's Tax Code

Foreword by Marcos Motta

The Beautiful Game's Tax Code

The practical guide to the essential principles of taxation in professional football

Panagiotis Christos Roumeliotis and Mario Tenore

This book has been informed, in part, by work conducted through Delian Consulting, a Switzerland-based fractional private office coordinating independent professionals who support professional athletes in Europe with wealth planning, financial structuring, and cross-border advisory. The firm's approach is designed to help athletes grow, preserve, protect, and ultimately transfer their wealth, securing long-term financial continuity and peace of mind.

Panagiotis C. Roumeliotis: p.roumeliotis@hotmail.com
Mario Tenore: Mario.Tenore@studiopirola.com

Contents

Key Disclaimers

This book provides foundational insights into tax principles and concepts relevant to the football industry. Its primary purpose is to offer high-level guidance for agents, lawyers, and other professionals.

While this book serves as a practical resource for initial assessments and strategic discussions, it is not a substitute for detailed legal, financial, or tax advice. The examples and scenarios included are illustrative and designed to reflect typical cases. However, they may not comprehensively address all variables, jurisdictional nuances, or the complexities of cross-border arrangements.

Tax laws and regulations vary significantly across jurisdictions and are subject to frequent amendments or changes in interpretation. We have made every effort to ensure the accuracy and timeliness of the information presented. However, readers are strongly encouraged to verify the currency of the information and consult qualified professionals, including local tax advisors or legal experts, for tailored advice before making decisions or taking action based on the content of this book.

This book addresses tax principles and concepts broadly relevant across jurisdictions, with a primary focus on OECD-member countries. While the principles discussed are universal, their practical application may vary depending on local laws, regulations, and enforcement practices.

By understanding the principles outlined in this book, you will be well-equipped to engage in informed discussions and make strategic decisions in the dynamic world of football taxation.

The authors do not assume any liability for direct, indirect, incidental, or consequential loss or damage resulting from reliance on the content provided. Use of this book and its content is at the reader's own risk.

Panagiotis Christos Roumeliotis:

*"To my loving parents, Christos and Dimitra,
and my incredible siblings, Ektoras, Rafail, and Margarita."*

Mario Tenore:

*"To my wife Claudia, my daughters,
Gaia and Ambra, my parents and my brother"*

Foreword

In the complex world of international football, where talent transcends borders and clubs compete on a global scale, the transfer of players is far more than a simple "deal done." It is a complex environment comprising multiple verticals, with taxation playing a pivotal role that is often overlooked.

Understanding the intricacies of taxation in the international transfer of football players is not merely a matter for accountants or legal advisors, but essential for anyone invested in the sport's ecosystem.

Taxation, in this context, is a multifaceted force that influences decisions shaping the global football landscape. It impacts the economics of transfers, players' net earnings, and the competitive balance among clubs operating under different fiscal regimes.

Cross-border transfers introduce additional layers of complexity, including double taxation treaties, residency rules, transfer fees, image rights, and signing bonuses, each with distinct tax implications.

Navigating these regulations without guidance can result in substantial financial losses, reputational damage, and even complex legal disputes. Conversely, a better understanding of tax frameworks can allow strategic advantages, enabling clubs tooptimise their budgets while allowing players and agents to better strategize and illuminate their career paths. For scholars, it reveals the hidden mechanisms that shape the beautiful game.

This book delves into the critical yet underexplored domain of taxation in international player transfers, providing clarity on a subject. It bridges the gap between the technicalities of tax law and the practical realities of football's global market, equipping readers with the knowledge to navigate this intricate terrain, in an era where football's financial stakes are higher than ever, understanding taxation is not just a competitive edge but a necessity.

This reading is a timely and essential guide, shedding light on how fiscal policies intersect with the ambitions and transactions that shape the international football landscape. May it inspire a deeper understanding of the sport's global engineering and empower all those who engage with it to make decisions that are as strategic as they are passionate.

Marcos Motta, 12 May 2025
Founding Partner of Bichara e Motta Advogados

Testimonials

- **Rafaela Pimenta - Football Agent and Lawyer**

In international football, where transfers and contracts increasingly span multiple jurisdictions, taxation is one of the most complex and often fragmented areas professionals must navigate. What the book "The Beautiful Game's Tax Code" seeks to achieve is higher clarity and a practical guide to connects the dots. It brings structure, insight, and hands-on value to a space that truly needs it. A valuable resource for many of us.

- **Prof. Juan de Dios Crespo Pérez, LL.M.; MA - Ruiz-Huerta & Crespo**

Sports Lawyers When Panos and Mario asked me to write a testimonial on their book, my first thought was that I did not know anything about tax law and sport, but then I became aware that even with that ineptitude I have been surrounded by taxes even with no consent from my side.

And yes, indeed, in my quite 40 years in this hectic world of sport, mostly in the football side, I have encountered multiple issues regarding taxes. The most important one had been the transfer of Neymar Jr. from Barcelona FC to Paris-Saint-Germain and the key point was if the buy-out clause that exists in the Spanish Professional Sport Athletes Law was net or gross from a fiscal point of view.

The French club hired me to deal with that, and not being a specialist, the need of such a command drove me, years before that month of August 2017, to dig on it. And I wrote an article, much in advance of the payment of the 222 million Euros clause, stating that the clause shall be considered as net of any taxes. So, the job was easy...

But the multiple transactions that I have done in my career have shown me theabsolute necessity of understanding the muddy world of international taxes. Who must pay, how much, in which country, what documents are needed, and a large etc. This long and winding road is where our good fellows Panos and Mario have marvellously guided us and I cannot recommend more this book, which is THE tool that any sports lawyer might have on his table. So, as Woody Allen put it in his well- known movie, EVERYTHING YOU WANTED TO KNOW ABOUT SEX, SORRY, ABOUT SPORTS TAXES, AND YOU WERE AFRAID TO ASK, here you have. Enjoy it and thanks to the authors.

- **Michele Colucci – Member of the FIFA Football Tribunal**

In the context of international transfers of professional football players, tax considerations are of paramount importance, shaping the strategic decisions of both clubs and athletes. While contractual and regulatory aspects often take centre stage, it is the tax dimension that frequently determines the real economic and legal viability of a deal. Navigating issues such as tax residence, double taxation treaties, and tie-breaker rules requires not only technical knowledge but also a strategic outlook. This book provides a valuable starting point for professionals seeking to assess and manage the fiscal implications of cross-border transfers. It is a practical and insightful resource for anyone involved in the global football industry.

- **Erkut Sogut – Sports Lawyer, Founder & CEO of The Football Week**

Panos and Mario have done a great job with The Beautiful Game's Tax Code. Taxation in football can be complicated and intimidating for anyone in the business. This book simplifies things; it explains important tax issues clearly and provides practical advice that you can use straight away. It's genuinely helpful, easy to follow, and directly addresses the real-life scenarios we face in our daily work. Highly recommended.

- **Sébastien Ledure – Managing Partner, CRESTA**

In international transfers, dealing with multiple jurisdictions and time constraints are two of the key challenges we face as legal advisors to elite players. Being able to count on local experts as Mario Tenore and Panagiotis Roumeliotis is of the essence. Their effort to compile such valuable, unique and time-saving guide as "The Beautiful Game's Tax Code" deserves all praise. I am sure it will be a priceless tool to all practitioners worldwide.

- **Daniel Geey – Sports Partner, SHERIDANS**

Navigating the financial and contractual intricacies of modern football is no easy task, and 'The Beautiful Game's Tax Code' delivers exactly what industry professionals need; a practical, experience-driven field manual. From international transfers to image rights structuring, this book unpacks the complexities with clarity, insight, and real-world relevance. A must-read for agents, sports lawyers, and advisors shaping the future of football's financial landscape.

- **Luis Villas-Boas Pires – Head of Agents, FIFA**

If you have any questions or concerns about any tax related matters in football, then Panagiotis and Mario are the ones to reach out. This book is a testament to their expertise and knowledge in a such an intricate and difficult area as tax in professional football. By using practical examples, they contribute to a better understanding to the principles of taxation in professional football. Congratulations to them for putting all their time and energy into producing this book!

- **Konstantinos Antoniou - Partner, MCA Sports Law LLP (Doha, Qatar), Senior Advisor, Qatar Football Association (Doha, Qatar)**

The Beautiful Game's Tax Code, co-authored by the distinguished colleagues Panagiotis Christos Roumeliotis and Mario Tenore, is an essential resource for practitioners in the modern football industry. In a legal environment where tax matters are often underestimated or misunderstood, this book fills a critical gap with clarity and practice-oriented guidance.

Having advised on numerous player transfers and contractual negotiations involving football players and clubs, coaches, and football agents across various jurisdictions, I can confirm that tax matters require specific attention and expertise. In today's professional football landscape, tax discussions can become a recurring point of contention in the negotiation of transfers and employment contracts, or even a deal-breaker. Tax issues are also decisive, often affecting the careers of athletes and coaches as well as the business choices of agents and clubs.

This book stands out for its practical approach. Instead of academic theory, the authors use real-life tax scenarios—through the fictional character Santiago Alvarado—to present and analyse key tax issues and suggest solutions.

For these reasons, and many others that you will also discover when you delve into it, this book is must-read. It equips lawyers, agents, clubs, and athletes with the tools to understand complex tax issues, negotiate more effectively, and ultimately make better decisions.

1. Introduction

In today's football industry, career-defining decisions are increasingly made off the pitch. Transfers, contracts, and endorsements define the game just as much as goals and victories.

According to FIFA's *Global Transfer Report* 2024[1], a record-breaking 78,742 international transfers were completed in a single year, a significant increase from the previous year. These figures highlight the importance of understanding tax implications in a globalized football market. Football has evolved into a global business, where deals involve navigating diverse tax systems, international treaties, and fluctuating regulations. These intricacies influence not just compliance but also negotiations, contracts, and the ultimate value of deals.

For the professionals at the centre of these transactions, a solid grasp of tax and financial structures can play the difference between a good deal and a great one. This book is here to close the knowledge gap. It goes beyond general advice to deliver practical strategies and real-world tools that help tackle these challenges head-on.

Whether you are negotiating contracts, managing a player's finances, or ensuring compliance with international tax laws, this book provides the basic knowledge and tools to excel.

---

1 https://digitalhub.fifa.com/m/142077cfbb75c2b0/original/Global-Transfer-Report-2024.pdf

1.1. Purpose of this Book

Taxation is a critical factor shaping modern football. It may determine where players sign, how contracts are structured, and the financial viability of transfers. For agents and lawyers, expertise in this area can turn an average deal into a career-defining success for their clients.

This book provides a concise, strategic guide to understanding football taxation, offering practical insights tailored to the realities of the sport. By bringing theoretical concepts with actionable tools empowers professionals to master high-stakes financial decisions.

By reading this book, you will:

- Gain confidence in complex scenarios: Understand dual tax residence conflicts, gross-up clauses, cross-border regulations, *etc.*
- Enhance negotiation strategies: Use templates[1], checklists, and decision-making frameworks for tax-efficient contracts.

This book's emphasis on practical application makes it a unique resource for professionals in the dynamic world of football taxation.

---

[1] The provided template clauses serve as a foundational starting point and must be tailored to the specific circumstances of the contract and the relevant jurisdictions. They are intended solely for educational purposes and should not be relied upon without review and approval by qualified legal and tax professionals. Adapting these templates to comply with applicable laws and regulations is essential to ensure their validity and enforceability.

1.2. Catered to Professionals

1.2.1. For Sports Agents

Think of this book as your **negotiation toolkit**. It provides you with the knowledge to manage players' tax risks and secure optimal deals. Whether negotiating gross-up clauses or signing-on bonuses, this book ensures you can advocate for your clients with awareness.

1.2.2. For Sports Lawyers

For lawyers, this book serves as a reference manual for drafting tax clauses in sport contracts. From image rights to indemnity clauses, the tax insights here will help you navigate complex cases.

1.2.3. For Professionals in Related Fields

Whether you are a student, academic, or professional working in adjacent fields like entertainment, this book provides universal lessons on tax intricacies in cross-border settings. It is a must-have resource for anyone exploring the intersection of global taxation and high-profile football careers.

1.3. Why Understanding Tax in Football Matters

Global football icons have faced audits and legal disputes over mismanaged image rights and hidden income streams. Clubs have struggled with complex tax obligations during high-value transfers.

Taxation has emerged as a defining factor in football, shaping player transfers, influencing club profitability, and affecting career direction. The stakes have never been higher - from hidden income streams to cross-border tax complexities.

Here is why tax is critical:

- High stakes: Mismanagement and non-compliance can result in fines, audits, or even criminal charges and tarnished reputations.
- Competitive advantage: Clubs and agents who master tax intricacies can negotiate better deals and attract top talents.
- Global complexity: With players frequently moving across borders, residency rules and double taxation treaties come into play.
- Alignment of priorities: Effective tax strategies align with broader legal, financial, and sporting goals.

This book equips you to address these challenges head-on, providing clarity where there is complexity by guiding you toward effective decisions.

1.4. Introducing Santiago Alvarado

Meet Santiago Alvarado, a fictional football star whose journey mirrors the real-world tax dilemmas players worldwide face. His story transforms tax scenarios into relatable, actionable insights for professionals.

Santiago Alvarado is a rising football star from Rosario, Argentina. After beginning his career at a local club, Atlético Rosario Juniors, his exceptional talent catches the attention of international scouts. At 21, he moves to State A to join a top-tier club, Real Catalonia FC. From his early years in Argentina to transfers across Europe, Santiago's journey illustrates the tax implications of residency rules, image rights, agency fees, and more.

Each chapter uses Santiago's story to explain tax concepts practically and provide actionable insights. Whether resolving a dual residency conflict between State A and State B or structuring a signing-on bonus under split-year rules, his journey offers relatable lessons for professionals.

1.5. A Note on Complexity and Practicality

Taxation in football is a challenging and ever-evolving field. While this book provides a comprehensive foundation, it is not a substitute for professional legal or tax advice. Laws change frequently - as does their interpretation - and every case is unique. This book simplifies complex scenarios for illustrative purposes, helping you grasp core principles and apply them confidently.

1.6. Embarking on the Journey

This book transforms *scattered insights* into a comprehensive guide, giving you the clarity and tools to make confident, informed decisions in football's dynamic tax landscape. By focusing on principles rather than exhaustive detail empowers you to tackle high-level problems confidently before seeking specialized expertise.

Get ready to explore the first comprehensive guide to football — practical, insightful, and tailored to your professional needs.

2. International Tax Basics

Effective tax planning can mean the difference between financial success and costly penalties in the high-stakes world of football transfers, where deals often involve millions of euros. Consider the case of a star player transferring to a new club mid-season: seemingly straightforward decisions like relocation timing or contract structure can trigger overlapping tax liabilities, residency conflicts, or double taxation - issues that can erode a player's net income.

For sports lawyers and football agents, mastering international tax principles is a competitive edge. Residency rules, double taxation treaties, and the interplay of cross-border earnings affect every transfer's financial structure, impacting players and clubs.

Tax planning is even more critical because the risks and liabilities may not always be immediately apparent. A poorly structured contract might seem harmless during negotiations but could reveal significant financial repercussions years later as jurisdictions audit historical tax compliance or when unforeseen regulatory changes occur. Without robust provisions addressing tax liabilities, professionals may face avoidable disputes, penalties, or unexpected tax burdens.

This chapter introduces the essential building blocks of international tax. We'll explore:

- Tax residency: Determining where a player is liable for tax and its implications.
- Worldwide vs. Territorial principles: How do different jurisdictions tax income and earnings?

- Split-Year treatment: Addressing mid-year changes in tax residency.
- Double Tax treaties: Resolving conflicts and avoiding double taxation.

These principles underpin effective negotiation and compliance in cross-border transfers. By mastering them, agents and lawyers can anticipate risks, design more thoughtful agreements, and provide long-term value to their clients.

2.1. Tax Residence

Tax residence is the cornerstone of international tax systems, dictating where players must declare and pay taxes on their worldwide income. For football professionals - who frequently move across borders - it defines their tax obligations and can drastically impact their net earnings.

Imagine a scenario where a player transfers mid-season. Without careful planning, they could become liable to pay taxes in their previous and new countries. This section breaks down:

- Definition of tax residence: A player's connection to a jurisdiction *via* physical presence, family, or economic ties.
- Global implications: How tax residency triggers obligations on worldwide income.

2.1.1. What is Tax Residence?

Generally, tax residence establishes a player's legal obligation to declare and pay taxes on their worldwide income. This obligation extends beyond wages to include bonuses, endorsements, and other earning. Determining tax residence is crucial because jurisdictions use varying criteria to define it, which can significantly impact a player's financial liabilities.

Days spent	Many countries apply a 183-day rule, where spending more than half the year in the country establishes residency.
Permanent home	Jurisdictions assess whether the player has an available residence within their borders that qualifies as a permanent home.
Family location	The presence of immediate family members, such as a spouse or dependents, often influences residency claims, especially in family-centered tax systems.
Economic interests	The jurisdiction hosting the player's working activity or his primary financial activities, such as investments or business operations, may claim residency.

Each jurisdiction applies these rules differently, and the assessment is made in each tax period. Therefore, a player's residency status can change frequently based on personal and professional circumstances. For example, transferring mid-season or relocating with family could trigger a reassessment of residency status. For agents and lawyers, understanding local residency criteria is key to advising clients effectively.

2.1.2. Can Tax Residence Change?

Yes, tax residence is dynamic and can change due to relocations or changes in personal circumstances. Football transfers, particularly mid-season moves, typically prompt residency reviews in multiple jurisdictions. Factors influencing a shift in tax residence include:

- Relocation timing: When players move mid-year, they may be eligible as tax residents in their departure and destination countries. This overlapping residency can result in two or more jurisdictions claiming taxing rights on the same income.

- Split-year rules: Some countries, like the UK, offer split-year treatment, allowing residency to be divided between jurisdictions within a single tax year. This can reduce dual taxation but requires careful documentation and planning.
- Varying tax periods: Different jurisdictions use varying tax periods for assessing residence. For example, the UK's fiscal year runs from 6 April to 5 April in the subsequent year, while most other countries use the calendar year. These discrepancies can complicate residency assessments.

Proactive planning is critical for professionals managing these moves to prevent overlapping liabilities and maximize tax efficiency.

2.1.3. Santiago Alvarado's Case

When Santiago Alvarado transferred from Argentina to State A at 21 in June 2025, he became subject to State A's 183-day residency rule. Spending more than 183 days in State A during the calendar year qualified him as a State A tax resident.

As a State A resident, Santiago was liable for tax on his worldwide income, including salary from his new club, Real Catalonia, and endorsement deals negotiated in State A.

This shift in residency status illustrates how relocation timing and residency rules directly impact a player's tax obligations.

2.1.4. Key Takeaways

- Tax residency determines the reach of tax obligations: A player's residency status significantly affects where and how much tax they must pay on worldwide income.
- Annual assessment: Residency is determined annually (generally in the calendar year) and can shift with relocations or changing circumstances.
- Timing matters: Align relocation dates strategically with fiscal years to optimize tax outcomes and avoid double taxation situations.

2.2. Worldwide vs. Territorial Principles

When taxing an individual, countries typically adopt one of two approaches: taxation based on residence or source of income. These principles form the foundation of international tax systems and directly impact how a player's earnings are taxed when they relocate or earn income across multiple jurisdictions.

Countries adopt two primary tax systems:

- Worldwide taxation (residence-based): Taxing residents on all global income - regardless of where it is earned.
- Territorial taxation (source-based): Taxing income only when it is earned within the country's borders.

Tax System	Example Jurisdictions	Key Principle	Practical Implications for Players
Worldwide Taxation	Spain, Germany	Taxes global income	Liability on endorsement income earned abroad
Territorial Taxation	Hong Kong, Panama, Uruguay	Taxes only income sourced in the country	No tax liability for foreign income

For footballers, the system applied directly impacts the tax burden on bonuses, salaries, and endorsement income.

2.2.1. Residence-based Taxation: Worldwide Income

On a residence basis, a country taxes an individual on their worldwide income -regardless of where it is earned (irrespective of the source). This is often referred to as having unlimited liability to tax, meaning that all global earnings are subject to taxation in the country of residence. However, there are exceptions, and most countries tax their residents only on income sourced locally.

2.2.2. Source-based Taxation: Territorial Income

Under the source basis, a country taxes only the income earned within its borders, regardless of the individual's residency status. This ensures fairness and parity with residents.

2.2.3. Santiago Alvarado's Case

For football professionals earning income in multiple countries, such as salaries, bonuses, and endorsements, the interplay between residence and source-based taxation can significantly impact their financial outcomes.

Santiago Alvarado relocates to State A and becomes a tax resident. He earns €2 million from his State A club (domestic income) and €500,000 in endorsement deals from State B (foreign income). State A taxes both income streams. However, through the State A - State B Double Taxation Treaty (DTT) in combination with the State A tax rules on the foreign tax credit, Santiago offsets taxes paid in State B (source country concerning the €500,000 endorsement income), reducing his total tax liability.

Generally, the residence state could grant relief in one of three ways:

- Exemption: Excludes foreign income from the taxable base in State A.
- Credit: Offsets taxes paid abroad (State B) against domestic liability (State A).
- Deduction: Reduces taxable income by the amount of foreign tax paid.

2.2.4. Key Takeaways

1. Residence-based taxation: Tax residents are generally taxed on their global earnings, reflecting their personal and economic ties to the jurisdiction.
2. Source-based taxation: Non-residents are taxed only on income earned within the source country.
3. Relief from double taxation: Countries use mechanisms like exemptions, credits, or deductions to avoid taxing the same income twice.

In the next section, we'll examine how split-year treatment addresses tax residence when a player relocates mid-year.

2.3. Split-Year Treatment

Mid-season transfers, a hallmark of football, often trigger significant tax implications. When a player relocates partway through the fiscal year, their tax residency status becomes a critical consideration. Such transitions can expose players to overlapping tax liabilities or compliance burdens across multiple jurisdictions without proper planning.

The split-year treatment provides a practical solution, allowing players relocating mid-season to avoid being taxed as full-year residents in both their origin and destination countries.

- Jurisdictions with split-year rules: Countries like the UK and France facilitate smoother residency transitions by adopting split-year treatment.
- Jurisdictions without split-year rules: Countries like Italy apply full-year worldwide taxation, even for mid-season relocations, which can easily lead to double taxation.

The latter approach ensures players are taxed proportionally based on their residency period, rather than their entire annual earnings when they arrive in or depart from a country mid-year.

2.3.1. How Split-Year Treatment Works

Split-year treatment divides the fiscal year into two distinct periods, ensuring that taxation is proportionate to the player's residency status. In jurisdictions like the UK, this involves:

- Before residency change: The player is taxed as a non-resident, with only income earned locally subject to taxation under source-based principles.
- After residency change: The player is taxed as a resident, with worldwide income becoming taxable for the months they qualify as a resident.

2.3.2. Santiago Alvarado's Case

2.3.2.1. Santiago's One-Season Stay in State A

During the 2025 summer transfer window (August), Santiago joined a State A team, Real Catalonia FC, spending 153 days in State A during the calendar year. Santiago avoids State A tax residency for the 2025 tax year as he falls below the 183-day threshold (*i.e.*, he spent only 153 days in State A that year, falling short of the residency threshold)[1]. Consequently:

- Santiago remains a non-resident in State A for the 2025 tax year.
- Non-residents in State A pay a flat 24%[2] tax rate on State A-sourced income, significantly lower than the 45% progressive rate for residents.
- By strategically timing his transfer, Santiago avoids significant tax liabilities.

If Santiago leaves State A in June 2026 for another club abroad, he will again spend less than 183 days in the country, avoiding tax residency for 2026 as well.

---

[1] For the purposes of this example, reference is made solely to the 183-day rule as the determining factor for tax residency. This assumption is based on the fact that Santiago does not meet the 183-day threshold, having spent only 153 days in State A. Additionally, it is presumed that he has neither a spouse nor dependent children residing in State A, nor does he maintain any significant economic interests, such as business operations or investments, apart from his salary earned during his employment.

[2] Tax rates referenced in this book are used for illustrative and indicative purposes only. Actual income tax liabilities are typically calculated using progressive tax systems, where different portions (tranches) of income are taxed at different rates, rather than a single flat rate. As such, the effective tax burden may differ materially from the examples provided. Additionally, specific tax outcomes depend on jurisdictional rules, available deductions, social security contributions, and other personal financial circumstances. Readers should consult qualified tax advisors for tailored assessments.

2.3.2.2. *Santiago's Transfer to State B*

Santiago signs with AC Lombardia Stars and relocates to State B in July 2026. State B's tax residency rules stipulate that an individual is considered a tax resident if they meet any of the following alternative criteria for more than 183 days in the year:

- Registered in State B's population registry.
- Domiciled in State B (centre of personal relations).
- Habitual abode is in State B.
- Physical presence.

Since State B does not allow split-year treatment, Santiago becomes a State B tax resident for the entire calendar year if he meets either criterion in 2026. This means:

1. His salary from Real Catalonia FC (earned January through June) is taxable in State B.
2. To avoid double taxation, he must claim relief through the State A — State B DTT in combination with State B tax credit rules, offsetting taxes already paid in State A. The lack of split-year treatment in State B may result in higher administrative burdens and even higher taxation.

2.3.2.3. *Santiago's transfer to State C*

After two seasons in State B, Santiago signs for a State C team on 1st July 2029 and relocates to State C with his family. State C offers split-year treatment, meaning:

1. Santiago's worldwide income becomes taxable in State C only from the date he establishes tax residency (July 2029), whilst State B remains responsible for taxing his pre-relocation earnings.
2. For the first half of the year (January–June), he is taxed only in State B on income earned there as non-resident.

If Santiago transfers again the following July 2030, he would:

- Be treated as a tax resident of State C only until July 2030.
- Be subject to source-based taxation for income earned in State C after July 2030 (presumably as non-resident).

2.3.3. Key Takeaways

1. Mid-season transfers require careful planning to navigate residency thresholds and tax obligations.
2. Understanding whether the destination country applies split-year treatment or requires full-year taxation.
3. Coordinating relocation dates to optimize clients' tax positions and avoid unnecessary and/or unexpected tax liabilities.

Let's now explore the role of double tax treaties in resolving cross-border tax conflicts.

2.4. Double Tax Treaties and Dual Residence: Conflict Resolution

When a player simultaneously maintains personal or economic ties to one jurisdiction while relocating for work to another, they may inadvertently become a dual tax resident. This scenario often arises during cross-border transfers, where players retain homes, families, or business and financial interests in one country while working in another. Dual residency exposes players to overlapping tax liabilities and administrative complexities, posing significant financial risks if not carefully managed.

DTTs are the cornerstone of resolving dual residency conflicts. These bilateral agreements harmonize taxation rules between jurisdictions, ensuring players are not doubly taxed on their income. By defining taxing rights and providing mechanisms to eliminate or reduce the burden of double taxation, DTTs reduce financial and administrative risks for football professionals.

2.4.1. What are DTTs?

DTTs resolve cross-border tax issues by:

- Allocating taxing rights: Defining how income, capital, and gains are taxed across jurisdictions.
- Avoiding double taxation: Clarifying which country has the right to tax a specific item of income.
- Mitigating tax avoidance and evasion: Promoting transparency and cooperation between tax authorities.

Often based on the OECD Model Tax Convention, these treaties follow a standardized framework to address conflicts. However, DTT provisions do not apply automatically. Players must actively claim treaty benefits by providing documentation, including:

- Tax residency certificates: Evidence of residency in a treaty jurisdiction.
- Proof of foreign tax payments: Records showing taxes paid in the source jurisdiction.

2.4.2. Resolving Dual Residence Conflicts: Santiago Alvarado's Case

Santiago Alvarado's mid-season transfer from State B to State C illustrates the complexities of dual tax residency and the critical role of DTTs in resolving such conflicts. His case highlights the challenges for footballers face when balancing professional commitments with personal and financial ties across jurisdictions.

2.4.2.1. Permanent Transfer from State A to State B

In January 2026, during the mid-season transfer window, Santiago signs a two-year contract with AC Lombardia Stars in State B, departing from his prior club, Real Catalonia FC, in State A. While Santiago relocates to State B for his new role, his family remains in State A, where they reside in the family home. Beyond his salary, Santiago also earns endorsement income from a brand in State A and continues to manage real estate investments in State A.

These factors trigger a dual residency conflict:

State A's claim: State A tax authorities could argue Santiago remains a tax resident due to:

- The presence of his family in State A.
- Ownership of the family home.
- Economic ties, including endorsement income and real estate investments.

State B's Claim: State B authorities could assert Santiago's tax residency based on:

- Spending over 183 days in State B due to his employment with AC Lombardia Stars.

Such a conflict requires applying the State A - State B DTT to determine Santiago's primary tax residency.

Tie-breaker resolution: Applying DTT criteria

The State A — State B DTT employs a structured sequence of tie-breaker rules to resolve dual residency disputes. Santiago's case is resolved as follows:

Permanent home	Santiago maintains homes in State A and State B, making this criterion inconclusive. Both residences are available to him during the tax year.
Center of vital interests	State A authorities could emphasize Santiago's family and economic ties to State A, including his ongoing investments and endorsements. Conversely, State B authorities could prioritize Santiago's professional ties as a player for AC Lombardia Stars, alongside his day-to-day presence in State B.
Habitual abode	Santiago spends over 183 days in State B during the tax year, indicating a stronger habitual connection to State B.
Nationality	If the above criteria were inconclusive, Santiago's Argentinian nationality could have been considered. However, the habitual abode criterion may resolve the conflict in favor of State B.

Outcome: residency determination

Based on the DTT's tie-breaker provisions:

- Primary tax residency: Santiago may be deemed a State B tax resident for the 2026 fiscal year.

- Spanish obligations: State A may retain the right to tax State A-sourced income, such as endorsement payments. Relief for double taxation is provided in State B through the DTT's credit method in combination with State B tax credit rules, ensuring Santiago avoids paying taxes twice on the same income.

2.4.2.2. Temporary Transfer (loan) From State A to State B

Loan agreements introduce unique tax challenges in football, when players temporarily transfer between clubs across borders. These scenarios raise critical questions about tax residency and wage allocation, requiring careful analysis of several factors:

- Structure of the loan agreement: Clarity on which club (parent or loan) pays wages.
- Duration of the loan: The loan's length can impact the player's residency status and tax obligations.
- Applicable DTTs: The availability of relief mechanisms to mitigate double taxation.

These considerations shape the financial outcomes for players, clubs, and agents. The following scenarios provide practical insights into managing tax implications for long-term and short-term loans.

2.4.2.3. Scenario 1: Payment by the Loan Club

In a typical loan arrangement, the parent club suspends its employment relationship, and the loan club assumes full responsibility for paying wages.

Example: In January 2026, Santiago is loaned from Real Catalonia FC (State A) to AC Lombardia Stars (State B) for one year. AC Lombardia Stars pays 100% of Santiago's wages during this period.

Key Tax Implications:

1. **Change in tax residency:**

    - Santiago relocates to State B and spends more than 183 days there, establishing State B as his primary tax residence for 2026. It should be assessed, though, whether he retains State A tax residence.
    - As a State B tax resident, Santiago is subject to State B's progressive tax rates on his worldwide income.

2. **Tax withholding in State B:**

    - State B, as the source country, withholds income tax and social security contributions to Santiago's wages.
    - Calculation:
      Assuming an annual salary of €2,000,000 and a 45% tax rate (including local surcharges):
      €2,000,000 × 0.45 = €900,000 (State B tax withheld at source).

3. **Double taxation relief:**

    - State A retains the right to tax Santiago's residual income sourced there, such as income derived from endorsement deals.
    - Relief is provided under the State A - State B DTT in combination with State B tax credit rules through the credit method.

Example: If State A taxes €500,000 endorsement income at 20%:

- State A tax: €500,000 × 20% = €100,000.
- State B tax on the same income: €500,000 × 45% = €225,000.
- Relief: €225,000 – €100,000 = €125,000 (additional State B liability).

By applying DTT provisions in combination with State B tax credit rules, Santiago avoids double taxation while complying with laws in both jurisdictions.

2.4.2.4. Scenario 2: Partial Payment by the Parent Club

In an alternative arrangement, the parent club pays part of the player's wages while the loan club covers the rest.

Example: In July 2026, Santiago is loaned from Real Catalonia FC (State A) to AC Lombardia Stars (State B) for one season. During the loan period, AC Lombardia Stars pays 70% of Santiago's wages (€1,400,000), and Real Catalonia FC continues paying the remaining 30% (€600,000).

Key tax implications:

1. **Tax residency:**
    - Santiago spends more than 183 days in State B, establishing it as his primary tax residence. It should be assessed whether he retains State A tax residence
    - State A retains the right to tax wages paid by Real Catalonia FC.
2. **Source-based taxation:**
    - Wages paid by AC Lombardia Stars (State B):
        - State B, as the source country, taxes the €1,400,000 paid by AC Lombardia Stars.
        - €1,400,000 × 0.45 = €630,000 (Italian tax withheld).

- Wages paid by Real Catalonia FC (State A):
  - Although duties are performed in State B, State A, as the source country for these wages, taxes the €600,000 paid by Real Catalonia FC.
  - €600,000 is taxed in State A at 20%, generating €120,000 liability.
  - The same income is also subject to taxation in State B under its worldwide income rules. Relief mechanisms under the State A – State B DTT are applied to prevent double taxation.

3. **Double Taxation Relief:**

- State A taxes paid on €600,000 wages are credited against the State B tax liability:
  - State B tax on €600,000: €600,000 × 45% = €270,000.
  - Relief: €270,000 – €120,000 = €150,000 (remaining State B liability).

Total tax liability:

- State B wages: €1,400,000×0.45=€630,000.
- Tax related to State A wages taxable in State B (after credit): EUR 150,000
- State A wage: €120,000.
- Total tax liability: €630,000+€270,000=€900,000.

2.4.2.5. Short-term Loan Arrangements

Short-term loans (typically less than 183 days) create unique tax scenarios, as players often retain tax residency in their home country.

Example: In July 2026, Santiago is loaned from Real Catalonia FC (State A) to AC Lombardia Stars (State B) for six months, with the loan concluding on January 15, 2027, aligned with the winter transfer window.

Key tax implications:

1. **Tax Residency**

    - State A: Santiago retains his State A tax residency under the 183-day rule for 2026, as he spends most of the year (January to July) in State A and maintains substantial personal and economic ties there.
    - State B: As the source country, Italy taxes Santiago only on income earned during his loan period.

2. **Source-based Taxation in State B**

    - Santiago earns €1,000,000 during his loan period in State B.
    - As the source country, State B withholds tax on the income earned while Santiago is playing for AC Lombardia Stars.
        - State B tax calculation: €1,000,000 × 45% = €450,000 (tax withheld at source).

3. **Double Taxation Relief**

    - As Santiago's country of residence, State A taxes his worldwide income, including wages earned in State B. However, relief is provided under the State A-State B DTT to avoid double taxation.
        - State A tax liability: Assume State A's tax rate on worldwide income is 45%.

    - Credit calculation: Taxes paid in State B (€450,000) are credited against the State A tax liability on the same income:
        - State A tax on €1,000,000: €1,000,000 × 45% = €450,000.
        - Relief under the DTT: €450,000 – €450,000 = €0 (additional State A liability).

Total tax liability for the Loan Period

- State B tax (withheld at source): €450,000.
- Additional State A tax liability (after credit): €0.
- Total: €450,000.

2.4.3. Key Takeaways

- Early residency planning: Assess tax residency risks at the outset of transfers or loans. Anticipate dual residency claims by understanding the 183-day rules and the center of vital interests in both jurisdictions.
- Strategize transfer timelines: Align transfer dates to avoid unnecessary and/or unexpected tax burdens. For short-term loans, ensure players spend less than 183 days in the host country to retain home tax residency.
- Define wage payment responsibilities: Clarify in contracts whether the parent or loan club is responsible for withholding and remitting taxes.
- Tax withholding clause: Detail which club deducts and remits taxes for income earned in the host country.

2.5. Relief Methods in DTTs

DTTs provide essential mechanisms to eliminate or mitigate the financial burden of double taxation, ensuring players can manage cross-border earnings efficiently. The three primary relief methods - Exemption, Credit, and Deduction - each address double taxation differently, with varying financial implications depending on the countries' tax systems and rates.

Method	Taxable income in residence country	Total tax lability	Notes
Exemption	Only local income	Low	Excludes foreign income entirely, offering the most favorable outcome.
Credit	Global income	Moderate	Credits taxes paid abroad against domestic liability, ensuring fair burden allocation.
Deduction	Reduced global income	High	Reduces taxable income by foreign tax paid but offers less relief than other methods.

2.5.1. Exemption Method

The Exemption Method excludes foreign-sourced income from taxation in the player's country of residence. This method is particularly advantageous when the exemption is full, as it removes the foreign income entirely from the taxable base in the Residence State. However, some jurisdictions implement the exemption with progression variation, where foreign income is considered solely to determine the applicable tax rate for domestic income.

2.5.1.1. Santiago Alvarado's Case

Santiago Alvarado, a State B tax resident, earns:

€1,500,000 salary from AC Lombardia Stars (State B-sourced income).

Income tax band	Income tax rate
Up to €1, 500,000	15%
Equal or exceeding €1 ,500,001	30%
Equal or exceeding €2 ,000,001	40%

€500,000 rental income from a property in State A (State A-sourced income, taxed at 20%).

Scenario 1: Full exemption method

Under the full exemption method, Santiago's €500,000 rental income is excluded from State B's taxable base, leaving only his State B-sourced salary subject to tax therein. The rental income would be subject to tax in State A.

State B taxes only the €1,500,000 salary: €1,500,000 × 15% = €225,000.

State A taxes the €500,000 rental income: €500,000 x 20% = €100,000

- Total tax liability: €225,000 + €100,000 = €325,000

Scenario 2: Exemption with progression method

Assume a country (State B) applies the exemption with progression method. Santiago's €500,000 foreign income is included only to determine the progressive tax rate applied to his State B income (*i.e.*, Santiago's progressive tax rate increases to 30% due to the inclusion of his €500,000 rental income), although it is not actually taxed.

Step 1: Determine the progressive rate

- Total worldwide income: €1,500,000 (State B's income) + €500,000 (State A's income) = €,2,000,000.
  - €1,500,000 x 15% = €225,000
  - €500,000 x 30% = €150,000
  - Total: €375,000

Then the tax bill is reduced by a proportion that corresponds to the amount of his foreign income as a proportion of his worldwide income:

€500,000/€2,000,000 x €375,000 = €93,750

Tax payable in State B: €375,000 - €93,750 = €281,250

Tax payable in State A: €500,000 x 20% = €100,000

- Total tax liability: €281,250 + €100,000 = €381,250

The exemption with progression increases Santiago's tax liability by €56,250 compared to the full exemption method. This occurs because the higher worldwide income raises the applicable progressive tax rate from 15% to 30%, even though the foreign income remains exempt.

2.5.2. Credit Method

The Credit Method offsets taxes paid abroad against the player's tax liability in their country of residence. Unlike the exemption method, foreign income is included in the taxable base, but the method ensures that the player does not pay tax on the same income twice.

2.5.2.1. Santiago Alvarado's case

Santiago Alvarado, a State B tax resident, earns the following during the tax year:

- €1,500,000 salary from AC Lombardi Stars (State B-sourced income).
- €500,000 endorsement income from a State A brand (State A-sourced income, taxed at 20% in State A).

Tax Calculation:

Step 1: Determine the tax liability in State B

- State B taxes Santiago's worldwide income at a progressive rate of 43%.
- Total worldwide income: €2,000,000 (State B and State A income).
- State B tax liability on worldwide income: €2,000,000×43% = €860,000.

Step 2: Credit for State A tax paid

- State A tax on endorsement income: €500,000 × 20% = €100,000.
- State B grants credit for the €100,000 paid in State A, reducing Santiago's State B tax liability: €860,000 – €100,000 = €760,000.

Total Tax Paid

- Tax Paid in State A: €100,000 (on endorsement income).
- Tax Paid in State B: €760,000 (after applying the foreign tax credit).
- Combined Tax Liability: €860,000 (43% of total worldwide income, ensuring no double taxation).

By using the credit method, Santiago avoids double taxation, effectively paying €100,000 in State A and €760,000 in State B.

2.5.3. Deduction Method

The deduction method treats taxes paid abroad as a deductible expense, reducing the taxable base in the residence country. While this approach offers relief, it is generally less advantageous than the exemption or credit methods because it does not directly offset the tax liability, resulting in a higher overall tax burden.

2.5.3.1. Santiago Alvarado's Case

Using the exact figures:

Tax Calculation:

Step 1: Foreign tax paid in State A

- State A tax on endorsement income: €500,000 × 20% = €100,000.

Step 2: Deduct foreign taxes paid from State B taxable base

- Total worldwide income: €2,000,000.
- Deduct foreign taxes paid in State A: €2,000,000 – €100,000 = 1,900,000 (adjusted taxable income in State B).

Step 3: Calculate tax in State B

- State B taxes Santiago's adjusted taxable income at a progressive rate of 43%: €1,900,000 × 43% = €817,000.

Total Tax Paid

- Tax paid in State A: €100,000.
- Tax paid in State B: €817,000.
- Combined tax liability: €917,000.

The deduction method reduces Santiago's taxable base in State B but does not provide a full offset for taxes paid in State A. Compared to the credit method, Santiago's combined tax liability is €57,000 higher (€917,000 *vs.* €860,000).

The full exemption method has the lowest tax liability, while the deduction method is the least beneficial. The credit method provides an effective mechanism to avoid double taxation while maintaining tax equity.

2.6. Tax Residence Risk Score Tool

The tax residence risk score tool is designed to assist professionals in assessing dual residency risks for football players transferring between jurisdictions. It provides a structured checklist of factors, assigning weighted scores to predict the likelihood of dual residence conflicts. This tool helps anticipate potential issues, enabling better planning and compliance with applicable tax rules.

Risk assessment table

Factor	Description	Score (0–5)
Days of presence	Number of days the player spends in each jurisdiction. (>183 days = high risk)	
Permanent home	Availability of permanent homes in one or both jurisdictions. (Multiple homes = higher risk)	
Economic ties	Strength of financial ties (e.g., salary, investments, property) to each jurisdiction.	
Social & family ties	Location of immediate family, dependents, or strong personal connections.	
Employment or economic ties	Clarity and location of employment contract and primary duties. (Ambiguity = higher risk)	
Split-year rules	Does the destination country apply the split-year treatment? (Yes = lower risk)	
Treaty tie-breaker	Strength of financial ties (e.g., salary, investments, property) to each jurisdiction.	
Social & family ties	Is there a clear resolution mechanism in the relevant Double Tax Treaty? (Yes = lower risk)	

Scoring guide

- 0–10: low risk
  Straightforward planning: minimal intervention required.
- 11–20: moderate risk
  Review tie-breaker rules and document economic/social ties carefully.
- 21–30: high risk
  Immediate action needed.

How to use the tool

- Evaluate each factor: Assign a score (0–5) based on the player's circumstances for each factor.
- Calculate total score: Sum the scores across all factors to determine the risk category.
- Action plan: Use the scoring guide to decide on the level of intervention required.

3. Taxation Systems and Image Rights

Having explored how DTTs help resolve dual residence conflicts and mitigate tax burdens, it's equally critical to understand the domestic taxation systems that players encounter throughout their careers. Every financial and income component is impacted - from wages to endorsement income.

This chapter begins with the distinction between PAYE (pay-as-you-earn) and self-assessment, two core methods for taxing football salaries and bonuses.

We then dive into the realm of image rights companies (IRCs), a popular yet increasingly scrutinized tool for managing endorsement income. As international rules evolve, the benefits and risks of IRCs demand careful consideration. Finally, we explore how alternative tax regimes in countries like Italy[1], and France are designed to attract top talent, offering lucrative incentives to players willing to relocate.

3.1. PAYE and Self-Assessment Explained

Football players encounter two primary taxation systems based on the type of income they earn:

- PAYE: The employer (*e.g.*, football clubs) automatically deducts taxes when the player's salary is paid. This system simplifies compliance for regular earnings like wages and bonuses.

[1] Till 31 December 2023.

- Self-Assessment: For income streams outside traditional payroll, such as endorsement deals, rental property income, or business income, the player must declare and pay taxes directly. This system places the *onus* on the player to report accurately and manage compliance.

Both systems are critical in managing a player's tax obligations, particularly for those with diverse income streams.

3.1.1. Comparison between PAYE and Self-Assessment

Aspect	PAYE	Self-Assessment
Who manages taxes	The employer deducts income tax and submits it to authorities	The player is responsible for calculating and submitting taxes.
Complexity	It is straightforward for players; the employer handles most obligations.	Requires detailed record-keeping, tax expertise, and proactive planning for compliance.
Payment schedule	Taxes are deducted monthly at the source.	Taxes are paid in lump sums, typically once per year.
Additional income	Does not account for external income like sponsorship deals.	Requires the declaration of all global income, including endorsements and non-salary earnings.
Best for	Players with simple income structures and limited additional income streams.	Players with diverse income sources or those with tax-deductible expenses like agent fees.

3.1.2. Decision Tree: PAYE vs. Self-Assessment

This decision tree guides football players in effectively identifying the applicable taxation system for their earnings and planning tax compliance.

3.1.3. Santiago Alvarado's Case

In his debut season at AC Lombardia Stars, Santiago deals with both two taxation systems, the PAYE for his salary and the self-assessment process for his endorsement income:

- PAYE on salary:

Santiago earns a €3,000,000 salary, fully taxed in State B under the PAYE system. State B applies a 45% tax, resulting in €3,000,000 × 0.45 = €1,350,000 (tax withheld at source).

- Self-assessment on endorsement income:

Santiago receives an additional €600,000 from a State A brand for endorsement deals. This income is subject to taxation in State A as the source country and State B as his tax residence. However, relief under the State A - State B DTT prevents double taxation:

- State A tax (source-based): €600,000 × 0.20 = €120,000.
- State B tax liability before credit: €600,000 × 0.45 = €270,000.
- Relief (State A tax credited): €270,000 – €120,000 = €150,000.

Total tax liability:

- State B salary taxes: €1,350,000.
- Endorsement income taxes: €120,000 (State A) + €150,000 (State B) = €270,000.

Santiago's total tax bill for the year amounts to €1,620,000, efficiently managed through applying PAYE and self-assessment rules and treaty-based relief mechanisms.

3.2. Image Rights and Tax Strategy: The Role of IRCs for Football Players

In modern football, where players' brands often rival or surpass their clubs in global marketability, managing image rights has become a cornerstone of financial strategy. The IRC constitutes a specialized structure that allows players to separate their commercial income, such as sponsorships, endorsements, and branding deals, from their employment income. When structured correctly, IRCs can unlock significant tax efficiencies and provide a platform for players to capitalize on their global appeal.

But with opportunity comes responsibility. IRCs are under increasing scrutiny from tax authorities, particularly with the emergence of anti-abuse measures. Missteps can result in income reclassification, financial penalties, and reputational damage.

This section explores:

- The purpose and benefits of IRCs.
- Key compliance requirements and risks.
- Real-world applications and pitfalls.

3.2.1. Purpose and Benefits of IRCs

For elite footballers, commercial opportunities extend far beyond their salaries. Sponsorship deals, licensing agreements, and global brand partnerships generate significant revenue streams that, if structured correctly, can offer financial efficiency and long-term protection. IRCs provide a structured mechanism for separating a player's commercial income from their employment earnings. Beyond the tax advantages, IRCs also help safeguard assets and enhance financial organization. Below are the key benefits that make IRCs an essential tool for modern football professionals.

3.2.1.1. Tax Efficiency

One of the primary advantages of an IRC is the ability to route commercial income through a corporate entity, where corporate tax rates are often significantly lower than personal income tax rates, which can exceed 40-

50% in many jurisdictions. This structured approach legally optimizes tax efficiency, provided the IRC adheres to regulatory requirements and economic substance tests.

3.2.1.2. Commercial Focus

By centralizing a player's commercial activities, an IRC provides a straightforward, professional platform for handling endorsement deals, licensing agreements, and promotional engagements. For example, Santiago Alvarado's IRC could enter sponsorship agreements with international brands, ensuring that these transactions are managed separately from his club salary, thus reinforcing the legitimacy of his commercial income.

3.2.1.3. Asset Protection

Beyond tax efficiency, IRCs serve as a legal shield, protecting a player's image rights from potential liabilities, financial claims, or legal disputes. Given that a player's brand is one of their most valuable assets, an IRC ensures that these rights are structured, protected, and strategically monetized for long-term sustainability.

3.2.2. Tax Compliance Requirements

While IRCs provide significant financial and strategic benefits, their effectiveness depends entirely on strict compliance with tax regulations. Tax authorities closely scrutinize IRCs to ensure they are genuine commercial entities rather than artificial structures designed solely for tax avoidance. Failure to comply can lead to tax audits, penalties, and even income reclassification as employment earnings, negating any financial advantage, not to mention the criminal liabilities

To operate legally and effectively, an IRC must meet the following key compliance requirements:

3.2.2.1. Commercial Rationale

Agreements between the IRC and the football club must reflect genuine business transactions rather than mere tax reduction mechanisms. This means:

- The IRC's activities must be distinct from the player's employment contract.
- Licensing agreements must be adequately documented and clearly define the player's commercial exploitation rights scope.
- The club's payments for image rights must align with market norms to avoid challenges from tax authorities based on a disguised salary claim.

3.2.2.2. Arm's Length Pricing

Payments made to an IRC to use a player's image rights must comply with transfer pricing principles, ensuring that transactions between related entities - such as a player and their personally owned IRC - are conducted at fair market value. This applies at two critical levels:

1. Between the Player and the IRC (Licensing Agreement):

    - The IRC must compensate the player appropriately for acquiring the rights to exploit their image.
    - The fee must be consistent with what an independent entity would pay for a comparable licensing agreement.
    - Tax authorities may argue that the player is shifting taxable income to a lower-taxed corporate structure if the licensing fee is set too low.

2. Between the IRC and External Parties (Club/Sponsors):

- When the IRC licenses the player's image rights to clubs, brands, or sponsors, the fees must also be set at arm's length rates.
- The valuation should be based on comparative deals for similar players with equivalent marketability and commercial reach.
- Overstating the value could trigger tax reclassification of excess payments as disguised salary.

Key compliance risks:

- IRC underpaying the player: If the IRC pays the player an unreasonably low fee for image rights, tax authorities may disregard the structure, arguing that the income should be taxed as direct employment income.
- IRC overcharging Clubs: If the IRC invoices clubs at inflated rates, authorities may challenge the legitimacy of the income split, potentially reclassifying a portion as employment earnings.

Best Practice:

- Establish a market-based licensing fee for the player's IRC using benchmarking studies and industry comparisons.
- Maintain documentation justifying valuations, demonstrating commercial rationale for the chosen figures.
- Regularly review and update agreements to reflect the player's evolving market value.

3.2.2.3. Economic Substance

An IRC must demonstrate actual business activity that is in line with international tax standards designed to prevent the use of shell entities. This requires:

- Qualified personnel managing commercial contracts.
- A physical office in the jurisdiction where the IRC is registered.
- Active management of sponsorships, licensing deals, and brand engagements.

If an IRC lacks economic substance, tax authorities may disregard it as a legitimate entity and classify its income as direct personal earnings, eliminating any tax advantage.

3.2.2.4. Proportional Income

The income generated by an IRC must be reasonable and proportional to the player's actual marketability and commercial engagements. Tax authorities benchmark income levels based on the following:

- Comparable endorsement earnings of other high-profile players.
- The player's publicity value, media presence, and endorsement history.
- The real contribution of the IRC to managing commercial agreements.

Excessive payments to an IRC beyond what are commercially justifiable may be flagged for reclassification as personal income, subjecting it to standard employment tax rates.

3.2.3. Regulatory Challenges and ATAD 3

The Anti-Tax Avoidance Directive 3 (ATAD 3), proposed by the European Commission in 2021, aims to combat the misuse of shell companies - entities that generate passive income without substantial economic activity. Since many IRCs derive income from royalties, licensing agreements, and commercial deals, ATAD 3, if adopted, may present significant regulatory challenges for footballers utilizing these structures. Please note that domestic tax systems are often equipped with domestic rules that aim to achieve the same or similar goals as ATAD 3. Therefore, you should always consult a local tax advisor to monitor the risk of audit or tax assessment.

This section outlines the directive's key provisions, compliance requirements, and practical implications for football players leveraging IRCs.

3.2.3.1. Background and Legislative Context

ATAD 3 remains currently under negotiation. Once and if finalized, EU Member States must transpose the directive into national laws, setting an enforcement timeline. While the exact implementation date is uncertain, players and advisors must prepare in advance to avoid disruptions in their tax structures.

The directive reinforces that companies must demonstrate genuine economic activity, preventing artificial arrangements that shift income without substance. Failure to comply could result in severe consequences, including loss of tax treaty benefits, higher tax liabilities, and reputational risks.

3.2.3.2. Key Requirements Under ATAD 3

ATAD 3 introduces a "substance test" with strict compliance criteria to distinguish legitimate business operations from artificial tax structures. IRCs must meet these standards to avoid reclassification as a shell company:

1. Minimum substance requirements

To be considered a legitimate business, an IRC must demonstrate:

- Local employment: Having dedicated staff involved in actual business operations.
- Physical presence: Maintaining an office in its jurisdiction of registration.
- Decision-making independence: Ensuring the IRC makes strategic and commercial decisions, not outsourced entirely to third-party service providers.

2. Transparency and documentation obligations

IRCs must provide extensive documentation proving their legitimacy:

- Image rights licensing agreements: Structured contracts between the player and the IRC.
- Financial records: Evidence of operational expenses, payroll, and other business costs.
- Corporate governance: Board minutes, club agreements, and proof of business decision-making within the IRC.

3. Penalties for non-compliance

If an IRC fails to meet the substance requirements, severe tax consequences may follow:

- Reclassification of income: The IRC's income could be treated as the player's income, subject to higher individual tax rates.
- Loss of tax treaty benefits: The IRC may no longer qualify for EU tax directives, exposing it to higher withholding taxes and reducing overall tax efficiency.
- Tax audits and legal scrutiny: Non-compliance increases the risk of audits, financial penalties, and potential reputational damage.

3.2.3.3. Practical Implications for IRCs in Football

For football players utilizing IRCs, ATAD 3 introduces a heightened level of scrutiny and new compliance obligations. To safeguard against risks, players and advisors must:

- Conduct a compliance review: Ensure the IRC meets all substance and governance requirements.
- Invest in local operations: Hiring employees and maintaining an active business presence may be necessary to comply with the directive.
- Reassess image rights agreements: Contracts between the player, IRC, and external parties must reflect commercial reality rather than a tax-driven structure.
- Plan for future regulations: Given ATAD 3's broad anti-avoidance focus, long-term tax strategies should emphasize genuine economic activity over aggressive tax minimization.

3.2.4. Santiago Alvarado's Case

Santiago Alvarado establishes an IRC in State D to manage his commercial earnings, generating €1,000,000 annually from image rights agreements. State D's effective corporate tax rate of 5% offers a significant tax advantage compared to State A's progressive individual tax rate of 43%.

Santiago's structure is scrutinized by State A tax authorities based on the directive's proposed framework. Their assessment uncovers key compliance risks that could challenge the legitimacy of Santiago's IRC.

Compliance risks identified

1. Lack of operational presence

    - Santiago's IRC has no employees or physical office in State D, failing the economic substance test.
    - Without a local business infrastructure, such as staff, independent management, and active operations, the IRC could be deemed a shell entity, potentially resulting in a denial of tax benefits and reassessment by tax authorities.

2. Disproportionate income allocation

    - Santiago's image rights income (€1,000,000) accounts for 25% of his total earnings (€4,000,000) in State A, exceeding the State A safe harbor threshold of 15% (if any).
    - Under State A's current anti-avoidance rules, authorities could reclassify a portion of the IRC's income as employment salary, subjecting it to higher individual tax rates (up to 43%).

3. Lack of contractual separation

    - The absence of an explicit, independent licensing agreement between Santiago and his IRC weakens the commercial justification for the entity.
    - Tax authorities assess whether the IRC's licensing agreements, revenue streams, and management structure reflect genuine business activity or merely serve as a tax-driven mechanism.
    - Without a formal separation between employment income and image rights, Santiago's IRC could face reclassification, back taxes, and penalties.

Hypothetical outcome of a tax audit

Santiago's IRC could fail the proposed substance test, leading to significant tax and compliance consequences:

- Reclassification as a shell company
  If Santiago's IRC is deemed a shell entity, authorities may disregard its corporate structure and reclassify the income as personal earnings, fully taxable at individual rates. This would nullify any tax advantages from routing income through a corporate structure.

- Revised tax liability
  Under State D's corporate tax regime, Santiago's IRC benefits from a 5% effective tax rate, meaning his €1,000,000 image rights income is taxed at just €50,000. If reclassified under State A's tax regime, the same income would be taxed at 43%, leading to a dramatically higher tax burden:

  €1,000,000 × 43% = €430,000
  (Personal tax liability under State A rates).
  Increase in tax burden: €380,000.

- Additional compliance consequences

Loss of tax treaty protections: If the IRC is reclassified as a shell entity, it could lose access to tax treaty benefits, potentially triggering higher withholding taxes on international payments.

Audit and penalties: State A tax authorities could initiate backdated tax audits, impose interest charges on unpaid taxes, and levy penalties for misclassification of income.

Reputational risk: High-profile cases of tax reclassification can lead to public scrutiny, damaging Santiago's brand image and marketability for future endorsements.

While ATAD 3 remains a *proposed directive*, its provisions highlight the importance of proactively addressing substance and compliance issues to avoid significant future tax liabilities and reputational risks.

3.3. Key Takeaways

1. Tax efficiency

When structured correctly, IRCs allow players to separate image rights income from salary, benefiting from lower corporate tax rates and reducing overall tax liabilities.

2. Substance is essential

To avoid reclassification as personal income, IRCs must function as genuine business entities with the following:

- A physical office and operational infrastructure in their jurisdiction.
- Local management and qualified staff actively handling contracts.
- Demonstrable commercial activities, ensuring economic substance.

3. Regulatory compliance

Players and advisors must:

- Separate image rights income from employment income.
- Ensure payments comply with transfer pricing rules and reflect the player's market value.
- Maintain detailed records (independent valuations, licensing agreements, transfer pricing documentation) to support legitimacy.

4. Jurisdictional differences matter

IRC tax treatment varies significantly by country, requiring localized structuring. For instance, jurisdictions have different benchmarks for proportionality.

5. Market-based valuation of image rights

Payments for image rights must reflect genuine commercial value and be supported by:

- Player popularity and marketability metrics.
- Independent benchmarking and valuations to justify fees.
- Third-party assessments to withstand tax authority scrutiny.

6. Clubs' responsibilities and compliance

Clubs engaging with IRCs must ensure compliance, including:

- Justifying image rights payments with independent audits.
- Ensuring payments comply with local tax regulations.
- Monitoring the player's IRC for adherence to substance requirements.

Decision tree: "Are your image rights agreements compliant?"

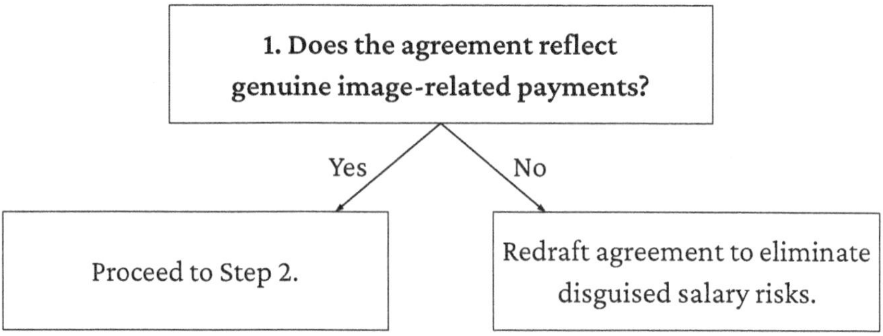

Red flag: If the agreement lacks a clear commercial rationale and mirrors a salary payment structure, it may be reclassified as employment income.

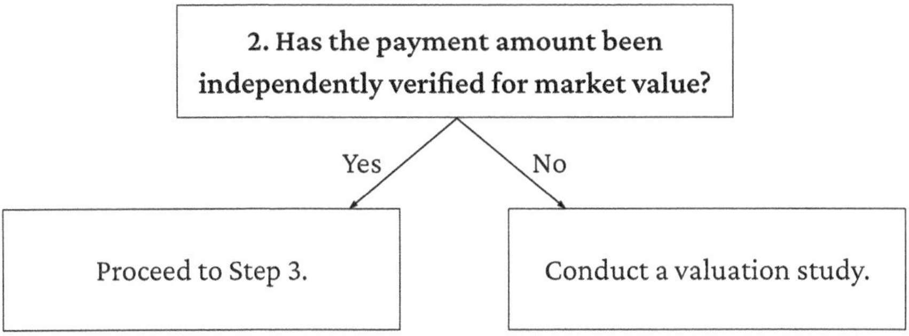

Tax authorities scrutinize inflated image rights payments. Independent valuations help prevent tax disputes.

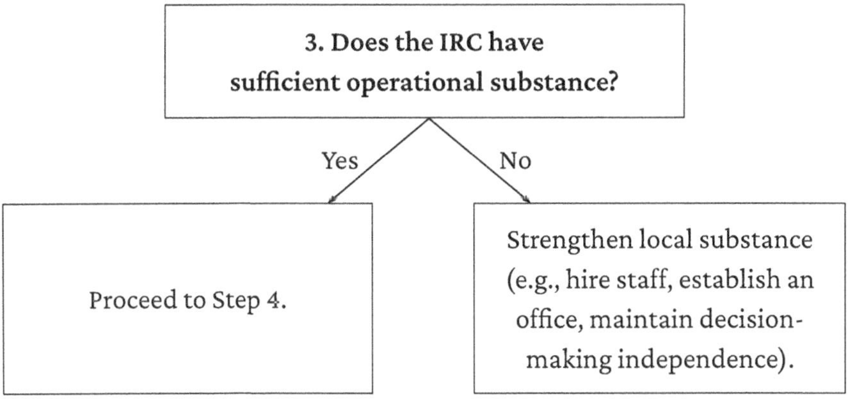

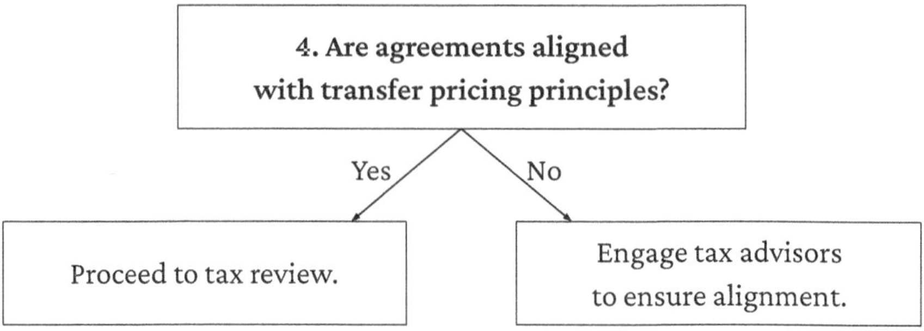

An IRC without real economic activity risks being classified as a "shell entity" under anti-avoidance rules.

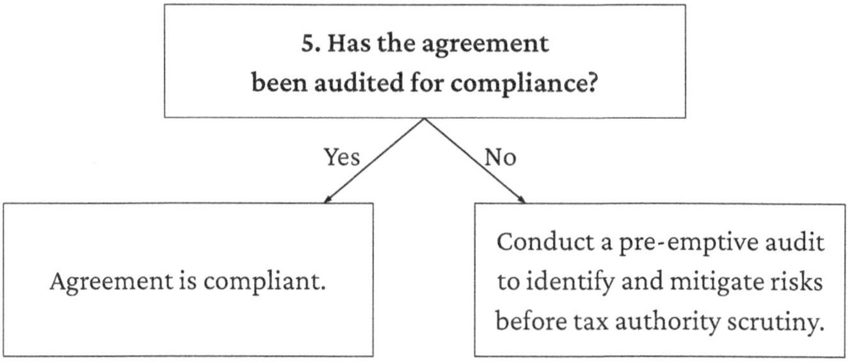

Image rights payments should reflect fair market value as negotiated between unrelated parties (arm's length principle).

4. Special Tax Regimes

Many countries implement special tax regimes to attract professional athletes by offering substantial tax reductions. However, these regimes come with strict eligibility criteria, and their benefits vary depending on income structure and residency status. Given the complexity and evolving nature of tax laws, professional tax guidance is essential to ensure compliance and strategic planning. While this section highlights examples from Italy and France, it does not provide a comprehensive legal analysis. Instead, it illustrates how such regimes function and how they may be leveraged for tax optimization in football.[1]

4.1. Italy's Special Tax Regimes

Before 2024, Italy implemented two distinct tax regimes aimed at attracting professional sportspersons and high-net-worth individuals to relocate to the country. The "Impatriate Regime" and the "Flat tax Regime" offer tailored tax incentives that can significantly reduce a player's tax liabilities, depending on income structure and source. While both regimes

[1] This section offers general illustrations of special tax regimes for athletes in select jurisdictions, such as Italy and France. It is not an exhaustive analysis of any specific tax framework, nor does it constitute tax or legal advice. Tax laws and incentives are subject to frequent changes and vary significantly across jurisdictions. Players, agents, and advisors should consult qualified tax professionals for a jurisdiction-specific, case-by-case assessment tailored to the player's individual circumstances. The information presented is for educational purposes only and is intended to provide conceptual insight rather than prescribe definitive tax strategies.

aim to enhance Italy's competitiveness in attracting international talent, they serve different purposes and apply to distinct income categories.

- The Impatriate regime provided tax exemptions on Italian-sourced earnings.
- The flat tax regime offers a flat tax on foreign-sourced income.

4.1.1. Impatriate Regime (Abolished as from 2024)

The Impatriate Regime offered significant tax incentives for players relocating to Italy. Under this regime, Italian-sourced income, including players' salaries, qualified for a 50% tax exemption.

To qualify, individuals must not have been Italian tax residents for at least two years before their relocation. They were required to maintain tax residency in Italy for at least two consecutive years to avoid a clawback of the tax benefits. The regime typically applied for five years, with potential extensions under specific conditions, such as having dependent children or purchasing property in Italy.

4.1.2. The High-Net-Worth Individuals' Regime

Italy continues to offer a flat tax regime for high-net-worth individuals relocating to the country, enabling significant tax savings on foreign-sourced income and gains. Under this regime, eligible individuals may opt for a flat annual income tax of €200,000 on all foreign-sourced income and profits, regardless of the amount earned abroad. However, domestic income and certain capital gains – such as those from foreign shareholdings exceeding specified thresholds – remain subject to Italy's standard progressive taxation rules (although the taxpayer may avoid such capital gain tax through a ruling procedure).

This regime is particularly attractive for players with substantial foreign earnings but requires careful consideration of the income structure and financial circumstances to determine its suitability. Factors such as the proportion of income earned domestically versus abroad and the geographic locations of professional activities play a critical role in evaluating the regime's applicability.

Key advisory considerations

- A comprehensive evaluation of the player's income structure, including income sources and geographic distributions, is essential to determine whether the regime offers optimal tax advantages.
- The regime's fixed nature may favor players with high foreign-sourced earnings (e.g., sponsorship deals from global brands). However, the exclusion of domestic income from the flat tax must be carefully considered during financial planning.

4.2. France's Impatriate Tax Regime

France's Inpatriate Tax Regime is designed to attract top professional athletes by offering substantial tax relief for up to eight years. This incentive allows foreign players relocating to France to benefit from significant employment and foreign-sourced income exemptions, reducing overall tax liabilities.

To qualify, sportspersons must:

- Not have been French tax residents for the five calendar years preceding their relocation.
- Establish their primary occupation in France, with employment linked to a French club or organisation.

Key Benefits of the inpatriate regime

1. 50% exemption on employment income from performances abroad

    - Applies to earnings linked to games, sponsorships, or activities conducted outside France.
    - Includes relocation bonuses but is subject to the "comparable salary test," ensuring salaries remain competitive yet aligned with local standards.

2. 50% exemption on foreign-sourced passive income

    - Covers dividends, royalties, and income from foreign investments.
    - Includes exemption from wealth tax on assets held abroad during the impatriation period.

5. Football Contract Clauses: Tax Nuances

While special tax regimes can offer significant advantages to footballers, the structure of their contracts ultimately determines how much of their earnings they retain. Every clause in a player's contract has tax implications, from salary arrangements to signing bonuses. Without careful structuring, even the most favourable tax regime can be undermined by poor contract drafting, unexpected liabilities, or residency conflicts.

This chapter shifts the focus from macro-level tax incentives to the micro-level intricacies of football contracts, equipping agents, clubs, and lawyers with practical strategies to ensure financial efficiency, compliance, and clarity in every contractual agreement.

This chapter covers:

- Net vs. gross salaries
- Gross-up agreements
- Termination provisions
- Signing-on fees and bonuses
- Tax indemnity clauses
- Agency commissions

5.1. Net vs. gross salaries: defining tax responsibilities in football contracts

Defining salary structures in the global football industry is essential to ensure financial predictability, compliance, and contractual clarity. One of the most critical distinctions in player contracts is between gross salary and net salary, which directly determine clubs' and players' tax obligations and financial responsibilities.

5.1.1. Definitions

- Gross salary: The total agreed amount before taxes, social security contributions, or any deductions. The player is responsible for their tax liabilities unless stated otherwise.
- Net salary: The player's final take-home pay after all taxes and deductions. When a contract specifies net salary, the club assumes responsibility for covering all applicable taxes in addition to the agreed amount.

This distinction has been the subject of arbitration disputes, particularly in cases where contracts lack explicit wording on whether a salary is gross or net. CAS rulings have repeatedly clarified these principles:

1. When "net salary" is explicitly stated, the club bears tax responsibility.

"It is a common understanding (...) in employment contracts between clubs and footballers that "net amount" refers to the final amount the creditor expects to receive in its bank account. Under this approach, all sorts of taxes, expenses, and charges due to the tax authorities or other third parties in connection with the payment, whether recoverable or not by the creditor, are to be paid by the debtor on top of the agreed net amount."

- *[CAS 2006/A/1018; CAS 2012/A/2806]*

This ruling establishes a clear precedent:

- If a contract explicitly states a net salary, the club is responsible for all related taxes
- The player assumes tax liability if the contract refers to a gross salary.
- Any ambiguity in contractual wording could result in disputes.

2. Good faith interpretation favors the player in case of ambiguity

"In the absence of an explicit reference, the player could have in good faith thought that such amount was to be considered as a net amount and that his good faith should be preserved."

- *[CAS 2015/A/3947; CAS 2016/A/4699]*

If a contract does not clearly state whether a salary is gross or net, arbitrators may rule in favour of the player, assuming they reasonably believed the amount to be net.

Practical implication:

- Clubs must draft contracts explicitly, avoiding vague salary terms.
- If a club intends for a salary to be gross, it must be clearly stated in the contract to avoid misinterpretation. For example:

"The Club agrees to pay the Player a gross annual salary of €[amount]. The Player shall be solely responsible for all applicable taxes, social security contributions, and statutory deductions under the laws of [jurisdiction]. The Club shall have no obligation to cover or reimburse any tax liabilities incurred by the Player unless expressly agreed otherwise in this contract."

3. Mixed labelling can lead to disputes

"When certain payments (e.g. bonuses) are explicitly stated as net, other payments (e.g., salary) not labelled are presumed gross."

- *[CAS 2016/A/4731]*

Suppose a contract labels some payments (such as signing bonuses) as "net" but does not specify the structure for other payments (such as base salary). In that case, arbitrators will likely interpret the unlabelled payments as gross. This underscores the importance of consistency in contract drafting to avoid interpretative conflicts.

These rulings highlight the importance of drafting precise contractual language to avoid ambiguity in net *vs.* gross salary discussions. Clubs and players must explicitly label all payments to ensure shared expectations and reduce the risk of disputes.

5.1.2. Impact of net vs. Gross salary clauses

Salary structures in football contracts significantly impact both players' take-home earnings and clubs' financial planning. Understanding the distinction between net and gross salary contracts is essential for optimising tax efficiency, ensuring contract clarity, and mitigating financial risks.

5.1.2.1. Net Salary Clauses (club covers taxes)

- Tax responsibility: The club covers all income tax, social security contributions, and statutory deductions, ensuring the player receives a fixed net amount.
- Higher cost for clubs: The club's total cost (gross salary) depends on tax rates, requiring careful budgeting.

- Financial predictability of players: The take-home pay remains unchanged, regardless of tax rate fluctuations.

Example: If a player negotiates a €2,000,000 net salary in a jurisdiction with a 45% tax rate, the club must pay the full €2,000,000 + applicable taxes (*e.g.*, € 3,636,363 gross total).

Risk mitigation strategy:

- Tax buffer clause: if tax rates increase, the club's liability is capped at a predefined threshold.

5.1.2.2. Gross Salary Clauses (Player Covers Taxes)

- Tax responsibility: The player must pay income tax, social security, and other deductions from their salary.
- Lower financial risk for clubs: The club's financial commitment does not change, regardless of tax rate fluctuations. The club's financial obligation is limited to the agreed gross amount.
- Variable take-home pay: Net earnings fluctuate depending on tax rates, deductions, and applicable reliefs.

Example: A €3,000,000 gross salary in a 45% tax jurisdiction results in a net take-home of approximately €1,650,000 after tax and contributions.

Risk mitigation strategy:

- Gross-up clauses: If net earnings fall below a certain threshold, the club compensates the player for additional tax liabilities.

5.1.2.3. Cross-border contracts: Key Challenges and Considerations

For Players

- Net salary contracts: Provide stability in high-tax jurisdictions. However, players must ensure their contracts account for potential future changes in tax rates or unforeseen liabilities.
- Gross salary contracts: Offer players control over tax planning but require proactive tax management to maximise take-home earnings. Players in particular assume responsibility for their tax obligations, which can significantly affect their net income, especially in high-tax jurisdictions. This often necessitates negotiating gross-up clauses to protect their earnings.

For Clubs

- Net salary contracts: Clubs must bear the burden of higher gross salary outlays in high-tax jurisdictions. Furthermore, they must plan for potential tax hikes, as they are responsible for covering tax liabilities.
- Gross salary contracts: Clubs limit financial exposure but may struggle to attract players to high-tax jurisdictions.

Factor	Net salary contract	Gross salary contract
Who pays taxes?	Club	Player
Take-home pay	Fixed	Varies with tax rates
Club's total cost	Higher (tax burden included)	Lower (fixed salary)
Financial risk for player	Lower (protected from tax hikes)	Higher (affected by tax changes)
Attractiveness for players	Lower in high-tax countries	Higher competitive in high-tax nations
Administrative burden	Higher (clubs handle compliance)	Lower (player files taxes)

5.1.3. Santiago Alvarado's Case

Santiago Alvarado moves from Real Catalonia FC (State A) to AC Lombardia Stars (State B), negotiating a net annual salary of €1,500,000. Because State B's Impatriate Tax Regime provides a 50% tax exemption on State B-sourced income, only half of Santiago's income is subject to taxation.

To determine the club's total financial obligation, we must calculate:

- Taxable income under the Inpatriate Regime
- The gross salary required to cover taxes and social security contributions (SSC)
- The employer's total financial commitment

Step 1: Determine Taxable Income

Since only 50% of Santiago's salary is taxable, his taxable income is:

Taxable Income=Net Salary×50%

Taxable Income=€1,500,000×50%=€750,000

Step 2: Calculate Gross Salary

The gross salary is determined using the effective tax rate, which accounts for both:

- Income tax: 43%
- Employee's social security contributions (SSC): 10%

Formula:

Gross salary = taxable income / 1 – (income tax rate + employee social security contribution rate)

Substituting values:

Gross salary = €750,000 / 1 – (0.43 + 0.1) = €750,000 / 0.47 = €1,595,745

Thus, to provide Santiago with a net salary of €1,500,000, AC Lombardia Stars must commit to a gross salary of €1,595,745, factoring in income tax and social security contributions.

5.1.4. Key Takeaways

- Always specify whether salaries are net or gross in contracts to avoid disputes. Clearly define who bears tax obligations, particularly in cross-border transfers, where tax treatment varies significantly.
- Engage tax professionals early in the contract negotiation to minimize tax risks and account for potential future tax law changes.
- Gross-up clauses are critical in high-tax jurisdictions, ensuring the player's net earnings remain stable despite tax fluctuations. Clubs must accurately estimate total financial obligations, considering the gross salary costs, employer and employee social security contributions, and additional compliance costs.
- Contracts should include mechanisms for tax adaptation, ensuring they remain effective amid regulatory changes. Consider post-termination risks. For example, deferred payments may expose players to higher future tax liabilities if they relocate to a higher-tax country.

5.2. Gross-up Agreements Securing Take-Home Pay: The Role of Gross-up Agreements

Understanding the distinction between net and gross salaries is crucial but ensuring that players receive the agreed-upon net amount requires additional safeguards. Given the complexities of cross-border taxation, fluctuating tax rates, and jurisdictional differences, clubs and players must implement mechanisms to mitigate financial risks. This is where gross-up agreements become essential.

Gross-up agreements are crucial in football contracts, ensuring players receive their full net salary without being impacted by unforeseen tax liabilities. These provisions are fundamental in high-tax jurisdictions and cross-border transfers, where tax obligations can be unpredictable and significantly affect a player's earnings.

5.2.1. What are Gross-up Agreements?

A gross-up agreement is a contractual provision that guarantees the player's take-home salary (*i.e.*, the net agreed-upon wage) remains constant, regardless of tax obligations. Under this arrangement, the club assumes responsibility for covering all income taxes, social security contributions, and other statutory deductions.

Gross-up clauses are particularly beneficial in international transfers, where players may face higher or unexpected tax liabilities due to differences in tax systems. Without gross-up agreements, players risk earning significantly less than expected after deductions, which can lead to contract disputes and dissatisfaction.

By implementing gross-up provisions, clubs create financial predictability for both parties, ensuring that contractual negotiations remain transparent and aligned with the tax realities of the player's country of employment.

5.2.2. Structuring Gross-up Clauses

A well-drafted gross-up clause provides financial certainty for players and mitigates risks for clubs by addressing critical tax-related scenarios. It ensures players receive their promised net salary while preparing clubs for additional obligations.

Gross-up clauses must also account for jurisdiction-specific legal and tax nuances. For example, some jurisdictions impose restrictions on agreements that shift tax liabilities entirely to employers, while others may have mandatory sharing of social security contributions. Moreover, the tax-deductibility of grossed-up payments varies across countries, potentially influencing the financial feasibility of these arrangements. Engaging local tax advisors ensures gross-up clauses are enforceable and aligned with local regulations.

5.2.2.1. Key Steps for Structuring Gross-up Clauses

1. Account for current tax obligations

Gross-up provisions must account for existing tax rates during contract execution.

2. Account for future tax rate changes

Contracts must account for potential future tax rate increases or new levies introduced during the agreement's term. This ensures the player's net pay remains unaffected, but the club's financial responsibility increases.

To balance financial certainty for players with risk management for clubs, gross-up clauses can include a gross-up ceiling, capping the employer's liability at a pre-agreed percentage of the player's base salary. A renegotiation clause may also provide flexibility if tax rates increase beyond a certain threshold, allowing both parties to revisit and adjust the agreement. For example, *'If the applicable tax rate increases by more than 10% during the contract term, the parties agree to renegotiate the gross-up terms to ensure fairness and sustainability.'* Such provisions protect clubs from excessive exposure while preserving the player's financial interests.

3. Cover additional liabilities

Gross-up clauses should extend beyond income tax to cover additional costs that could impact the player's salary.

(i) Social Security Contributions (SSC)

- In many countries, employers are responsible for mandatory SSC, which significantly increase the total cost of employment, though they do not reduce the player's gross or net salary.
- In jurisdictions where SSC is split between employer and employee, the employee portion is deducted from gross salary. If the player's contract specifies a net salary, the club must gross up the employee SSC to preserve the intended net income.

The employer's share of SSC is a separate legal obligation and must be considered in the club's total cost planning — but it is not part of the gross-up calculation. Tax authorities may reclassify certain benefits as taxable income, increasing tax exposure for the player.

- Signing bonuses, loyalty bonuses, housing, relocation costs, and travel benefits may be considered taxable benefits.
- The gross-up clause must ensure the club covers any unexpected tax liabilities due to reclassification.

4. Plan for Post-Termination Payments

Gross-up clauses should also account for payments made after the termination of the contract, especially when players relocate to jurisdictions with higher tax rates.

5. Draft separate agreements where necessary

In certain jurisdictions, gross-up clauses must be explicitly referenced in the employment contract to be legally enforceable. An alternative side agreement may be necessary if the local legal system does not allow tax liability to be transferred fully to the club.

5.2.3. Santiago Alvarado's Case

Santiago's contract with AC Lombardia Stars specifies a monthly net salary of €200,000. Given the combined player-side tax rate in State B is 53% (comprising a 43% income tax and 10% employee-side social security contribution), the club must determine the gross salary required to meet this net commitment.

Using the gross-up formula:

Gross Salary = €200,000 / 1–0.53 = €200,000 / 0.47 = €425,532

To ensure Santiago receives a net monthly salary of €200,000, AC Lombardia Stars must pay a gross wage of €425,532 per month, considering the 53% combined rate. In addition to the player's gross salary, the club must also account for the employer-side social security contribution (if applicable), which is a separate legal obligation. While it does not impact the player's net income, it represents a true financial cost to the club and must be considered for budgeting and internal cost planning purposes.

Tax-on-tax adjustment scenario

Beyond his guaranteed salary, Santiago is entitled to a €20,000 net taxable benefit (*e.g.*, housing allowance, or company car). To ensure he receives both his €200,000 net salary and this additional benefit net of taxes, the club must account for both income tax and employee-side social security contributions when grossing up (applying the same 53% combined tax rate to both). In this case, the applicable combined tax rate for the player is 53% (43% income tax + 10% employee SSC). This tax burden applies to both the base salary and the taxable benefit.

Key considerations:

- The club must ensure that Santiago's net salary (€200,000) remains intact.

The €20,000 taxable benefit must also be preserved in net terms, not eroded by taxes. A tax-on-tax effect occurs due to both amounts being grossed up simultaneously, increasing the overall cost. Applying the gross-up formula again, including the taxable benefit:

1. Grossing up net salary (base): €200,000 / 1−0.53=€200,000 / 0.47 = €425,532
2. Grossing up taxable benefit: €20,000 / 1−0.53 = €20,000 / 0.47 = €42,553
3. Total gross salary required: €425,532+€42,553=€468,085

This ensures both the net salary, and the taxable benefit are fully preserved after accounting for tax and employee SSC. Therefore, AC Lombardia Stars must pay a total gross monthly salary of approximately €468,085 to ensure Santiago receives both his net compensation and his benefit in full.

This approach reflects proper treatment of multi-component income and demonstrates how gross-up clauses must handle separate tax exposures per item, rather than aggregating all net values into a single gross-up formula.

5.3. Termination Provisions

Building on the importance of salary structuring, termination provisions represent another critical contractual element that can significantly impact a player's financial position. While gross-up agreements ensure players receive a fixed net salary throughout their contract, termination clauses determine what happens if the agreement ends prematurely.

These provisions typically encompass termination settlements, buy-out clauses, and liquidated damages clauses, which define each party's financial and legal obligations in such scenarios. However, the tax treatment of termination payments is a complex yet critical consideration that demands careful attention to avoid unintended financial consequences.

Termination payments are classified differently across jurisdictions, significantly impacting their tax treatment.

Ambiguities in drafting termination provisions can result in unintended tax burdens, disputes, and compliance risks for players and clubs. To avoid these pitfalls, it is essential to structure clauses precisely, ensuring clarity around the nature of payments and their tax implications. In the following sections, we will examine these provisions in more detail.

5.3.1. Termination Fees

Termination fees compensate players when their contracts end prematurely, typically due to mutual agreements, breaches, or unilateral terminations. These payments carry significant tax implications depending on timing, jurisdictional tax laws, and the player's residency at the time of payment. Precise contractual drafting prevents financial consequences and disputes for players and clubs.

Unlike liquidated damages clauses, which predefine financial consequences in the original contract, termination fees are often negotiated at the time of termination.

5.3.1.1. *Tax implications of Termination Payments*

The tax treatment of termination payments depends on how they are classified structured, and when and where they are paid. Poorly drafted termination provisions can lead to unexpected tax liabilities and reclassification risks. The following key factors must be considered:

1. Net *vs.* Gross payments:

It must be explicitly stated whether termination payments are net (after-tax) or gross (before-tax). Ambiguities can lead to disputes over who bears the tax burden, particularly in cross-border cases.

2. Tax residency at termination:

The player's tax residency at termination determines the applicable tax laws. If a player relocates post-termination, deferred payments could fall under the new jurisdiction's tax regime, potentially altering tax liabilities.

5.3.1.2. *Relevant CAS Case Law*

Arbitration rulings from the CAS provide valuable insights into the drafting, interpreting, and enforcing termination provisions. These cases highlight best practices for structuring termination payments to ensure tax efficiency and compliance:

1. Aris F.C. v. Sergio da Silva de Souza Junior (CAS 2006/A/1180)

    - Context: The contract was terminated by mutual agreement due to the player's injury, with a final settlement payment.
    - Ruling: The payment was deemed gross because the contract did not specify otherwise. The CAS relied on circumstantial evidence (such as non-round figures) to determine tax obligations.
    - Takeaway: Termination payments should explicitly state whether they are net or gross to avoid reliance on external evidence.

2. Del Bosque et al. v. Beşiktaş (CAS 2012/A/2760)

    - Context: Premature termination of a coaching contract, with compensation including net salaries and bonuses.
    - Ruling: An explicit net payment clause prevented disputes regarding tax liabilities. The ruling considered potential changes in tax residency between the termination and payment dates.
    - Takeaway: To avoid post-termination disputes, contracts should address potential tax residency changes and delayed payments.

3. Victor Javier Anino Bermudez v. Club Elazignspor Kulubu (CAS 2016/A/4699)

    - Context: The player terminated the contract with just cause and was entitled to grossed-up compensation.
    - Ruling: The net payment clause was enforced, requiring a gross-up calculation based on the player's tax residency.
    - Takeaway: Gross-up clauses ensure predictable financial outcome and tax compliance, particularly in cross-border disputes.

4. Udinese Calcio v. Morgan De Sanctis & Sevilla FC SAD (CAS 2009/A/1856)

    - Context: De Sanctis breached his contract prematurely, and the club sought to recover saved costs.
    - Ruling: CAS ruled that the gross-up of unpaid salaries should reflect the financial impact on the club, incorporating applicable tax rates.
    - Takeaway: CAS incorporates tax implications to ensure equitable remedies when assessing financial outcomes.

5.3.1.3. Santiago Alvarado's Case

Scenario 1: Santiago transfers in August and remains a State A tax resident

Santiago transferred from Real Catalonia FC (State A) to AC Lombardia Stars (State B) in August 2024. However, because State A does not apply split-year treatment, he remains a State A tax resident for the 2024 tax year. Upon termination, he receives a €500,000 settlement from Real Catalonia FC.

Tax treatment by jurisdiction

State A (Tax residence in 2024)

- As Santiago is deemed a State A tax resident for 2024, State A taxes his worldwide income, including the termination fee.
- The termination fee is classified as employment income since it is directly tied to the termination of his employment contract with Real Catalonia FC.
- Taxable income calculation:
    - Salary from Real Catalonia FC (January–August): €3,200,000 (€400,000/month).
    - Termination fee: €500,000.
    - Total taxable income in State A for 2024: €3,700,000.

- State A applies a progressive income tax system, with the top marginal rate at 45%.
- Tax calculation: €3,700,000 × 45% = €1,665,000 (total tax liability in State A).
- Tax liability on termination fee: €500,000 x 45%: € 225,000.

State B (non-tax resident status in 2024)

- Santiago does not meet State B's tax residency criteria in 2024, as he relocates in August and does not spend more than 183 days in State B during the tax year.
- State B does not tax the termination fee or other income Santiago earns before acquiring State B tax residency (non-residency impact).

Net termination fee

- Gross termination fee: €500,000.
- Tax in State A: €500,000 × 45% = €225,000.
- Net termination fee retained by Santiago: €500,000 – €225,000 = €275,000.

Warning: financial shortfall

1. Significant loss of income without gross-up protection:

Due to the omission of a gross-up clause in the termination agreement, Santiago could be personally liable for the €225,000 tax burden. This leaves him with only 55% of the agreed termination fee. This shortfall could have been avoided with a drafted clause specifying that the payment would be a net amount, obligating the club to cover the taxes.

2. Jurisdictional mismatch increases tax burden:

The lack of alignment with Santiago's tax residency exposes him to State A's high progressive tax rates, exacerbating the financial impact. If the payment had been deferred to a period when Santiago was a State B tax resident or of any other state, potential tax savings under State B's (more) favourable tax regime might have mitigated the burden.

3. Proactive drafting needed:

Termination clauses should explicitly define whether payments are gross or net. A gross-up clause ensures players receive the intended net payment, even when subject to high taxation.

Scenario 2: Santiago transfers in July and becomes State E tax resident

Santiago relocates to State E in August 2024, acquiring State E tax residency under the split-year rule. The €500,000 termination fee is paid in September 2024, following his transition to State E residency. This scenario highlights the challenges arising from cross-border taxation of termination fees, emphasizing the importance of timing, tax residency, and DTTs.

Tax treatment by Jurisdiction

State A (source country of the termination fee)

- State A retains taxing rights over the termination fee related to employment performed while Santiago was a State A tax resident.
- The State A tax authority imposes a 45% withholding tax on the €500,000 termination fee, amounting to €225,000.

State E (country of residence at the time of payment)

- Santiago became a State E tax resident in August 2024 under the split-year rule, which could make the State E his primary tax jurisdiction from that point onward (subject to the prescribed conditions being observed).
- As a State E tax resident, Santiago is taxed on his worldwide income from August 2024 onward. For this example, we assume that State E will levy tax on the €500,000 termination fee paid in September 2024 (this is hypothetical and must be assessed on an *ad hoc* basis, taking into account applicable domestic tax laws).

Key observations

1. Impact of timing:

The timing of Santiago's relocation to State E and the termination fee payment determines the applicable tax regime. Despite his State E residency status, the fee could remain subject to State A tax related to prior employment activities in Spain.

2. Potential risks:

Ambiguities in the timing of payment and tax residency status at the moment of payment can lead to disputes.

Warning: Financial Shortfall

As seen in Scenario 1, Santiago personally will absorb the tax burden (if any) because his contract does not specify gross or net payment terms. A gross-up clause would have required Real Catalonia FC to cover tax liabilities, ensuring he retained the full termination fee.

Scenario 3: Santiago transfers in January and becomes a State B tax resident

Santiago transferred to State B in January 2024, immediately acquiring State B tax residency. A €500,000 termination fee was paid to Santiago in February 2024.

This scenario presents a complex jurisdictional tax issue: whether State A retains taxing rights as the source country of the income or whether State B exercises its full taxation authority as Santiago's country of residence at the time of receipt. The outcome depends on interpreting domestic tax laws and the applicable State A-State B DTT.

Tax Treatment by Jurisdiction

State A (source country of the termination fee)

Whether the termination fee should be taxed in State A or solely in State B is debatable. If the payment is made after Santiago has established himself as a State B tax resident, the situation becomes less clear.

State A may argue that the termination fee relates to prior employment activities performed in State A, giving it the right to tax the payment despite Santiago no longer being a State A tax resident. However, since Santiago had already relocated to State B before receiving the payment, State A's right to tax the income could be challenged, shifting primary taxing rights to State A. If State A taxes the termination fee as State A-sourced income, the State A-State VB DTT will prevent double taxation through an exemption or a foreign tax credit.

State B (country of residency at the time of payment)

- State B taxes Santiago's worldwide income, including the termination fee, as he is a State B tax resident when the payment is reccived. Since Santiago is already a State B tax resident, when he gets the termination fee, State B taxes the full €500,000 payment.

5.3.1.4. Tax Optimization Strategy for Santiago and Key Takeaways

To maximize Santiago's net termination fee while ensuring compliance and minimizing tax burdens for both the player and the club, the following strategic considerations must be integrated into contract structuring:

1. Specify net or gross payments to avoid ambiguity

Specify whether termination payments are net or gross to avoid ambiguity and disputes. If net payment is agreed upon, the contract must include a gross-up clause obligating the club to cover all associated taxes, ensuring Santiago receives the full agreed net amount.

For example, "The Club guarantees that the Player shall receive a net termination payment of €500,000, with all applicable taxes, social security contributions, and withholding obligations borne by the Club."

2. Document gross-up provisions

A well-structured gross-up clause should account for current and future tax obligations. It should ensure that any tax rate increases do not erode the net amount due to Santiago and include provisions for unforeseen surcharges, penalties, or reclassification risks. In addition, it should clarify the treatment of fringe benefits (e.g., housing allowances, bonuses) to avoid unexpected taxation and ensure all employer-covered tax payments are also grossed up, preventing Santiago from bearing any hidden liabilities.

3. Address tax residency transitions

If termination payments are deferred or paid in instalments, define how each payment aligns with Santiago's residency status over time. Ensure that future tax obligations (e.g., post-relocation payments) are anticipated and addressed contractually.

5.3.2. Buy-out Clauses

Building on the discussion of termination fees, which are typically negotiated at the time of contract termination, buy-out clauses represent a different mechanism. They are fundamental provisions in football contracts that allow players to unilaterally terminate their agreements by paying a predetermined fee. These clauses clarify contractual relationships and facilitate player mobility, ensuring clubs receive compensation when a contract ends prematurely. However, the tax implications of buy-out payments can vary significantly depending on who makes the payment and how it is structured. This section explores the mechanics of buy-out clauses, and the relevant tax considerations.

5.3.2.1. How Buy-out Clauses Work

Buy-out clauses operate as a legally binding mechanism that allows players to secure their release from an existing contract by compensating the club for the value of their federative and economic rights. These clauses are negotiated when signing and serve as a safeguard for clubs while granting players greater control over their careers.

The buy-out process typically involves one of two scenarios:

- The player directly pays the buy-out fee.
- The acquiring club pays the fee on behalf of the player to facilitate a transfer.

5.3.2.2. Tax Implications of Buy-out Clauses

The tax treatment of buy-out clauses depends on who makes the payment and how jurisdictions classify the transaction. While buy-out clauses are designed to facilitate contractual freedom, their execution can trigger unintended tax liabilities. Below, we analyse the two primary scenarios:

Payment by the Player:

- When the player pays the buy-out fee from their personal funds, the payment is generally treated as a personal expense. While there are no immediate tax consequences, the funds used for the payment remain subject to standard income tax rules.
- For example, if a player uses salary or bonus earnings to cover the buy-out fee, those earnings would already have been taxed as employment income.

Payment by the new club on behalf of the player:

- In many jurisdictions, when a new club pays the buy-out fee directly, the payment may be deemed a taxable benefit for the player, making it subject to income tax.
- For the acquiring club, this could inflate the total cost of the transfer due to the gross-up required to account for tax liabilities.
- Clubs and players should carefully evaluate this scenario, as interpretations vary widely across jurisdictions, and tax authorities may scrutinize the nature of such payments.

5.3.2.3. Jurisdictional Example: Spain's 'Cláusula de Rescisión'

Spain's labour law provides a well-defined framework for buy-out clauses, known as the *'cláusula de rescisión.'* This statutory mechanism grants players the legal right to unilaterally terminate their contracts by paying compensation to their club. Unlike discretionary buy-out clauses in other jurisdictions, this provision is embedded in Spanish labour law, making it a fundamental aspect of contract negotiations in *La Liga* and beyond.

Key features:

- Players can legally terminate their contracts by paying a predefined buy-out or an amount determined by a labour court if not contractually stipulated.
- The mechanism is mandatory in Spain, meaning clubs must include a buy-out clause in every professional contract.
- Unlike standard buy-out clauses, which are privately negotiated, the Spanish system ensures enforceability under labour law, preventing disputes over the clause's right to execute.

Tax Treatment in Spain:

Spain's tax system treats buy-out clause payments differently from standard employment income, offering unique advantages:

- No reclassification as salary: Payments made by the acquiring club on behalf of the player are not considered employment income. Instead, they are classified as capital transactions, avoiding income tax liability for the player.
- Capital gain and capital loss offsetting:
  - The payment from the new club to the player is classified as a capital gain, representing the transfer of the player's economic rights.
  - When the player subsequently forwards the payment to their former club, it is treated as a capital loss, often resulting in a tax-neutral outcome.

- Buy-out fees in Spain are exempt from VAT, provided the documentation supports their classification as capital transactions rather than a taxable service.

5.3.3. Liquidated Damages Clauses

Liquidated damages clauses are integral to football employment contracts, establishing pre-determined compensation in unilateral termination or breach cases. These clauses promote financial predictability and contractual stability but bring nuanced legal and tax considerations that require careful drafting (*i.e.*, they should be formulated intelligibly, clearly, and robustly to reflect the parties' true intentions) and implementation.

Unlike termination fees, which are often negotiated at the time of termination, liquidated damages clauses are established at the contract's inception to outline the financial consequences of a potential unilateral breach.

5.3.3.1. Key Legal and Tax Considerations

At the heart of FIFA's Regulations on the Status and Transfer of Players (RSTP) is the contractual stability principle. Article 17 emphasizes the importance of allowing parties to define the nature and amount of compensation for early termination. Precise drafting minimizes ambiguity and ensures enforceability under FIFA regulations and CAS rulings. This foundational principle establishes the framework for liquidated damages provisions, but practical implementation requires understanding the governing legal framework.

Legal Framework: Swiss Law and the "Positive Interest" Principle

Swiss law often governs the interpretation of liquidated damages clauses in international disputes, especially where no governing law is specified in the contract. Swiss law adheres to the positive interest principle, which seeks to restore the injured party to the financial position they would have enjoyed had the contract been fully performed. This principle often necessitates grossing-up payments to ensure the stipulated net amount is delivered after applicable deductions. While the legal foundation is straightforward, tax considerations usually introduce additional complexity, mainly when a player's tax residency changes post-termination.

Tax Considerations: Residency and Cross-Border Implications

A player's tax residency at the time of payment significantly influences their tax liability.

For example, a player's relocation to a higher-tax jurisdiction post-termination can substantially increase the tax burden on compensation payments. Without contractual clarity, disputes may arise over who bears the additional tax costs arising from a change in tax residency.

To pre-empt such issues, contractual language must clearly outline the tax responsibilities of both parties. Ambiguities in liquidated damages clauses can undermine their effectiveness. To mitigate risks, contracts must explicitly specify:

- Net or gross payments: Define whether the compensation is net or gross. If net, the agreement should stipulate the need for gross-up calculations to account for tax liabilities.
- Tax residency: Address the player's tax residency at the time of payment to clarify applicable tax obligations.
- Applicable tax rates: Where feasible, specify the applicable tax rates or a requirement to account for future changes.

Even with explicit language, cross-border tax challenges necessitate further safeguards.

Players and clubs should ensure proper documentation to avoid double taxation, including Tax Certificates confirming withholding taxes paid at source. These documents are critical for claiming relief under applicable Double Tax Treaties (DTTs), minimizing disputes, and maximizing net compensation.

5.3.3.2. *Santiago Alvarado's Case*

Santiago Alvarado's contract with Real Catalonia FC includes a liquidated damages clause guaranteeing €200,000 (net) as compensation for early termination. Shortly after the termination, Santiago relocated to State B, a jurisdiction with a higher tax rate (43%) than State A (30%). The interplay between cross-border tax laws and contractual provisions creates a nuanced scenario with significant financial implications.

Key assumptions:

- Net liquidated damage amount: €200,000 net is guaranteed under the clause.
- Tax residency:
    - Santiago is a State A tax resident at the time of termination.
    - When the payment is made, Santiago is a State B tax resident.

- Applicable tax rates:
    - State A: 30% withholding tax.
    - State B: 43% income tax rate.

- A DTT exists between State A and State B to mitigate double taxation.

5.3.3.3. *Case 1: No Provision for Tax Residency*

If the contract does not account for Santiago's relocation and tax residency at the time of payment, the compensation is grossed up using State A's 30% tax rate, potentially causing a shortfall.

Tax calculations:

1. Gross-up (State A's tax rate): net amount (€200,000) / 1 – tax rate (0.30) = €285,714
2. Tax withheld in State A: €285,714 x 0.30 = 85,714
3. Taxes payable in State B: €285,714 x 0.43 = €122,857
4. Double taxation relief (State B provides a tax relief for taxes paid in State A): €122,857 - €85,714 = €37,143 (additional State B tax liability)
5. Net liquidated damages amount received: €285,714 - €85,714 - €37,143 = €162,857

Santiago receives €162,857 net, falling short of the €200,000 promised net compensation by €37,143 (18.6%). The oversight in accounting for Santiago's new tax residency and the higher State B tax rate causes this shortfall.

5.3.3.4. Case 2: Provision for Tax Residency

If the contract exlicitly considers Santiago's relocation and specifies gross compensation based on his tax residency at the time of payment, the shortfall can be avoided.

Tax calculations:

1. Gross-up (State B's tax rate) - the gross amount must consider State B's higher tax rate to preserve the net €200,000 compensation: net amount (€200,000) / 1 – tax rate (0.43) = €350,877
2. Taxes withheld in State A - State A, as the source state, taxes the liquidated damage sum: €350,877 x 0.30 = €105,263
3. Taxes payable in State B – State B taxes Santiago's worldwide income but provides a credit for taxes paid in State A: €350,877 x 0.43 = €150,877 (State B tax liability)
   Tax payable in State B (after credit): €150,877 - €105,263 = €45,614

4. Net amount received – after taxes in both State A and State B, Santiago's net income is: €350,877 - €105,263 - €45,614 = €200,000

With a properly structured gross-up clause considering Santiago's State B tax residency and State A's source-based taxation, the promised net €200,000 is preserved. However, the gross compensation required to fulfil this obligation increases significantly to account for taxation in both jurisdictions.

5.4. Tax Indemnity Clauses

Tax indemnity clauses are indispensable in modern football contracts, safeguarding parties, most often players, from unexpected tax liabilities arising due to the actions or inactions of another party, such as a football club. These provisions are especially critical in cross-border transfers, where overlapping jurisdictions and complex tax laws create heightened risks. Thoughtful drafting of tax indemnity clauses ensures financial predictability and mitigates potential disputes.

5.4.1. Key Features of Tax Indemnity Clauses

A well-designed tax indemnity clause is as much about foresight as it is about protection.

5.4.1.1. Purpose and Functionality

The foundation of a tax indemnity clause lies in its purpose: to distribute tax risks fairly between parties and protect the indemnified party from liabilities beyond their control. For instance, a player may face unforeseen claims if a club misclassifies income or fails to withhold taxes appropriately. By addressing such risks in advance, indemnity clauses ensure that the liable party assumes responsibility for their errors, fostering trust and contractual balance.

These clauses shield players from retrospective tax claims tied to signing-on fees or salaries that might be reclassified during a tax audit. On the other side, clubs also use these clauses to guard against liabilities arising from agents or intermediaries failing to comply with tax obligations. This mutual protection underscores the dual purpose of indemnity clauses in maintaining financial stability for all involved.

5.4.1.2. Practical Considerations

A well-drafted clause must clearly define the scope of liabilities it covers. These might include income tax, VAT, withholding tax (principal tax liabilities), related penalties, or interest.

Equally important is specifying the types of income protected, such as signing-on fees, image rights payments, salaries, or bonuses. This clarity prevents disputes by pre-emptively outlining the financial boundaries of indemnity.

As tax rules vary widely across jurisdictions, this makes it essential for indemnity clauses to adapt to the specific laws of relevant countries.

Tax compliance is a shared responsibility, and indemnity clauses should reflect this. Transparent reporting by all parties is crucial to avoid triggering indemnity claims unnecessarily. For instance, players must accurately declare their income in tax filings, while clubs must ensure proper tax withholding. This collaborative effort minimizes risks and reinforces the effectiveness of indemnity protections.

To ensure effectiveness and enforceability, indemnity clauses should include:

- A statute of limitations: Define a clear timeframe for tax claims (e.g., five years post-contract termination).
- Clear triggers: Specify events that activate indemnity, such as tax audits or reclassifications by authorities.
- Documentary requirements: Outline the evidence needed to support indemnity claims.

5.5. Signing-on Fees

Signing-on fees, often referred to as signing bonuses, are one-time payments made by a football club to a player when signing a new contract or transferring from another club. These payments play a crucial role in modern football, serving as powerful incentives to attract top talent, reward player loyalty, and demonstrate a club's intent to secure a player's long-term services. Unlike regular salaries or performance-based bonuses, signing-on fees are typically paid upfront or in agreed-upon instalments. They may include conditions such as completing a transfer or staying with the club for a specific period.

From a tax perspective, signing-on fees introduce unique challenges. Their upfront or conditional nature often triggers complex cross-border tax issues, especially in international transfers. These complexities arise because such payments must align with diverse tax rules, including residency criteria, DTTs, and the OECD's guidelines on taxing employment income.

5.5.1. A Key Principle Guiding the Tax Treatment of Signing-on Fees

Taxing signing-on fees presents a unique challenge, given the cross-border complexities often involved in professional football transfers. Understanding the fundamental principle governing the taxation of signing-on fees is essential for ensuring compliance.

According to the OECD Commentary on Article 15 (2014), the payout timing does not influence its taxability. A signing-on fee should be classified as employment income because it is directly linked to the player's future services under the new contract. This holds even if the payment is made before the official transfer date. The timing of a signing-on fee payment should not affect its taxability. Advisors should focus on how the fee is documented and connected to the contract rather than its payment date.

5.5.2. Santiago Alvarado's Case

Santiago negotiates a €2,000,000 signing-on fee paid upfront in January 2026 while transferring from Real Catalonia CF (State A) to AC Lombardia Stars (State B), with the move taking effect in July 2026.

If State B is determined to be Santiago's tax home for 2026, it will tax his worldwide income, while State A may only tax State A-sourced income. Even if Santiago had transferred in January 2026, State B would still have full taxing rights over his income (including the signing-on fee), as he would qualify as a State B tax resident for the entire year.

If State A wins the dual residence conflict, Santiago is treated as a State A tax resident for 2026. State A taxes his worldwide income whilst State B retains source taxing rights over the signing-on.

5.6. Percentage of a Future Transfer Fee

Negotiating a future transfer fee percentage represents a strategic component of many football contracts. This payment type can benefit the player significantly, but its tax treatment varies substantially depending on its classification and the jurisdictions involved. Whether categorized as employment income or investment income (capital gains), this payment has profound implications for tax rates, applicable laws, and double taxation relief under DTTs.

Classifying the future transfer fee percentage as either employment or investment income is a decisive factor in determining its tax treatment.

- Employment income: Payments linked directly to services rendered or obligations performed under an employment contract are typically classified as employment income. This classification subjects the payment to progressive tax rates and may include social security contributions.
- Investment income (chargeable capital gains): Payments structured as a share of economic rights or profits from future transfers may qualify as investment income (capital gains). This classification benefits from lower tax rates in some jurisdictions, such as capital gains treatment or reduced withholding taxes.

5.6.1. Santiago Alvarado's Case

In 2027, Santiago Alvarado transferred from Real Catalonia CF (State A) to AC Lombardia Stars (State B). As part of his employment contract with AC Lombardia Stars, Santiago negotiated a clause entitling him to 10% of any future transfer fee if the club sold him to another team. This clause became relevant in 2028, when AC Lombardia Stars transferred Santiago to Les Étoiles Olympiques (State C) for €20,000,000, resulting in a sell-on fee of €2,000,000 for Santiago.

The tax treatment of this sell-on fee depends on its classification, Santiago's tax residency in 2028, and the interaction of the State B-State C DTT.

Income classification

The classification of the sell-on fee as employment income or investment income determines its tax treatment in each jurisdiction (hypothetical assumptions):

- State B (source state):

The sell-on fee is derived directly from Santiago's employment contract with AC Lombardia Stars. State B classifies the income as employment income, as it is tied to Santiago's services and contractual obligations. Employment income is subject to State B's progressive income tax, with a top marginal rate of 43%.

- State C (residence state):

Santiago became a State C tax resident in July 2028 after transferring to Les Étoiles Olympiques. State C classifies the sell-on fee as investment income (capital gain), as it stems from negotiated contractual benefits. Investment income in State C is taxed at a flat rate of 30%.

Tax residency in 2028

State B: Santiago might cease to meet State B tax residency criteria following his transfer to State C in July 2028.

State C: Santiago could become a State C tax resident starting July 2028. Under State C's split-year rule, State C may tax his worldwide income earned during the latter half of the year.

Tax treatment in each jurisdiction

State B (source state): State B could tax the entire sell-on fee of €2,000,000 as employment income:

- Tax rate: 43%.
- State B Tax Liability: €2,000,000 × 43% = €860,000.

State C (residence state): State C may tax the sell-on fee as investment income under its worldwide taxation rules for July–December 2028:

- Tax rate: 30%.
- State C tax liability: €2,000,000 × 30% = €600,000.
- Double taxation relief: Under State B – State C DTT, State C could provide a foreign tax credit for taxes paid in State B. However, the credit would likely be limited to the amount of State C tax liability on the sell-on fee (€600,000):
  - State C tax credit: €600,000.
  - Net State C tax liability: €600,000 – €600,000 = €0.

Net retention from sell-on fee

- Gross sell-on fee: €2,000,000.
- Taxes paid: €860,000 (State B tax).
- Net retention: €2,000,000 – €860,000 = €1,140,000.

5.7. Agency Commission

Agency commission refers to the fee paid to an agent for representing a player in transfer or contract negotiations, including contract renewals. Depending on the agreement structure, the agent may be compensated by:

- The player (direct payment from earnings),
- The club (acting as a payer, on behalf of the player) or
- Both the player and the club (shared commission structures).

The tax implications of agency commissions vary across jurisdictions, influenced by factors such as:

- Payer classification (whether the payment is considered a deductible business expense or taxable income),
- Benefit-in-kind treatment (whether the club paying on behalf of the player results in taxable compensation for the player) and
- VAT and withholding tax obligations (particularly in cross-border transactions).

Historically, FIFA regulations permitted players to authorize clubs to pay agents directly, which created tax complexities, including potential reclassification of commissions as either a tax-deductible professional expense or a non-deductible benefit-in-kind. Additionally, agency commissions are often subject to VAT, requiring careful structuring to minimize double taxation risks.

This section examines these tax considerations through the lens of Santiago Alvarado's case and addresses legal uncertainties created by the evolving FIFA Football Agent Regulations (FFAR).

5.7.1. FIFA Football Agent Regulations (FFAR): Context and Temporary Suspension

On 16 December 2022, the FIFA Council approved the FIFA Football Agent Regulations (FFAR) to establish a balanced framework for the integrity of football transfers. However, coordinated litigation strategies led by agents and agents' associations across Europe resulted in the temporary worldwide suspension of specific provisions, pending a final decision from the European Court of Justice.

The suspended provisions include, amongst others:

- Service fee cap (Article 15, paragraphs 1–4).
- Rules on service fee payments (Article 14, paragraphs 6, 8, and 11).
- Client-pays rule (Article 14, paragraphs 2 and 10).

At the time of writing, these provisions remain unenforced globally. Therefore, this analysis focuses on the general tax fundamentals and prevailing practices before FFAR enforcement.

5.7.2. Why do Tax Rules Matter?

Tax rules governing agency commissions have significant financial implications for players, agents, and clubs. These rules affect how commissions are taxed, their deductibility, and the application of VAT. The following factors are particularly influential:

1. Tax treatment based on payer classification

The tax treatment depends on whether the player, the club, or both pay the agent's fee. When the club pays on behalf of the player, the payment may be treated as a taxable benefit-in-kind for the player, subject to payroll taxes and social security contributions. Some tax authorities require clubs to withhold taxes when making such payments.

In some jurisdictions, agency fees are classified as tax-deductible professional expenses, reducing taxable income for the payer (whether the club or the player). Other jurisdictions treat the payment as a non-deductible personal expense, increasing the tax liability for the player.

- Player-paid commissions:
    - It may be tax-deductible if classified as a professional expense, but some jurisdictions consider them non-deductible personal expenses.

- Club-paid commissions on behalf of the player:
    - Often treated as a benefit-in-kind, making them taxable as employment income and potentially subject to payroll taxes and social security contributions. Some tax authorities require clubs to withhold taxes when making such payments.

- Club-paid commissions for club representation:
    - If the agent represents the club's interests, the fee is typically a deductible business expense and not taxable for the player.
    - However, misclassification risks arise if the agent also acts for the player.

2. VAT rules:

Agency commissions generally attract VAT in the agent's country of residence. Cross-border payments may require the payer to self-account for VAT under reverse charge mechanisms.

5.7.3. Santiago Alvarado's Case

To illustrate the tax implications of agency commissions, consider the case of Santiago Alvarado, who transfers from Real Catalonia FC (State A) to AC Lombardia Stars (State B) on a three-year contract. As part of the transfer arrangement, Santiago's agent negotiated a 5% commission on Santiago's annual salary. For this example, we assume the following details:

- Santiago's annual salary is €200,000 (gross).
- The agent's commission is 5% of the annual salary, amounting to €10,000 (net of VAT).
- State B applies a VAT rate of 22%, which is charged on top of the agent's commission.
- Santiago's marginal personal income tax rate is 45%, applicable to all taxable income.

The club agrees to pay the agent's commission and VAT directly on Santiago's behalf. This payment triggers different tax implications depending on whether the agent's fee is classified as:

- A tax-deductible professional expense (neutral for Santiago).
- A non-deductible benefit-in-kind (increasing Santiago's taxable income).

5.7.3.1. Benefit in Kind Considered as a Tax-Deductible Professional Expense

In the first scenario, the agent's fee is considered a professional expense, which does not increase Santiago's taxable income. The tax treatment and outcomes are as follows:

1. Agent's commission + VAT:
    - Base commission (net of VAT): €10,000
    - VAT: €10,000 x 21% = €2,100
    - Total fee (commission + VAT): €10,000 + €2,100 = €12,100
2. Tax treatment:
    - Since the agent's fee is fully deductible, Santiago's taxable income remains at €200,000 (gross salary only)
    - Personal income tax is calculated solely on his salary: taxable income (€200,000) x 45% = €90,000
3. Net impact:
    - Santiago incurs no additional tax liability from the agent's fee
    - The club bears the full cost of the agent's commission, including VAT
    - Santiago retains his net salary of €200,000 - €90,000 = €110,000

4.2.2.1. Benefit in Kind Considered as a Non-Tax Deductible

In the second scenario, the agent's fee is classified as a benefit in kind, increasing Santiago's taxable income. The tax treatment and outcomes are as follows:

1. Agent's Commission + VAT:

    - Base commission (net of VAT): €10,000
    - VAT: €10,000 x 21% = €2,100
    - Total fee (commission + VAT): €10,000 + €2,100 = €12,100

2. Tax treatment:

    - The total fee of €12,100 is treated as a taxable benefit, increasing Santiago's total taxable income: €200,000 (base salary) + €12,100 (fringe benefit) = €212,100
    - Personal income tax is calculated on the increased taxable income: taxable income (€212,100) x 45% = €95,445

3. Net impact:

    - Santiago incurs an additional tax liability due to the benefit in kind classification
    - Santiago retains his net salary of €200,000 - €95,445 = €104,555

5.7.3.2. Key Takeaways

From the analysis of Santiago Alvarado's case, the following key takeaways emerge:

1. Tax-deductible *vs.* Non-deductible:

If the agent's fee is classified as a tax-deductible professional expense, Santiago achieves a higher net retention by avoiding additional taxable income. If the fee is treated as a non-deductible benefit-in-kind, Santiago's net retention decreases due to increased taxable income and corresponding tax liabilities.

2. Jurisdiction-specific rules:

Tax rules regarding agency commissions vary significantly across jurisdictions.

3. VAT implications:

The VAT portion of the agent's fee (21% in State B) also impacts the overall cost. Cross-border transactions require careful VAT handling to avoid unexpected tax liabilities. Both clubs and agents must ensure VAT obligations are correctly managed to maintain compliance.

6. Conclusion

After many years of working at the intersection of football and international tax, one learns that the problems are rarely dramatic, but they're often avoidable. Misunderstandings around net and gross payments, residency drift, or overlooked treaty relief rarely make headlines, yet they shape careers and relationships in lasting ways. What this book offers is a framework: a way to think about the structures, risks, and decision points that lie beneath the surface of every contract. The aim is not to overcomplicate, but to clarify and to help those advising players and clubs do so with precision, foresight, and confidence. In a world where so much moves quickly, good structure still matters.

Comprehensive Tax and Compliance Checklist for Football Professionals

Navigating tax compliance in football is as crucial as scoring goals on the pitch. With complex residency rules, cross-border contracts, and evolving regulations, players and agents must proactively structure agreements to optimize tax efficiency and avoid costly mistakes. This practical, step-by-step checklist provides football professionals, clubs, and legal advisors with a clear roadmap to mitigate risks, ensure compliance, and maximize financial security in international football transactions.

1. Residency and relocation planning

Action item	Details
Determine tax residency status.	Assess the player's current and future tax residency under local laws. Identify risks of dual residency under DTTs. Verify the applicability of the split-year treatment.
Assess social security implications.	Identify the applicable jurisdiction for social security contributions.
Track residency compliance	Maintain supporting documents (travel records, lease agreements, tax filings) to prove tax residency in case of audits.

2. Contract structuring

Action item	Details
Define gross vs. net salary terms	Clearly state if the contract is based on gross or net salary. If net, include a gross-up clause to cover tax liabilities.
Segregate income components	Differentiate salary, bonuses, signing-on fees, and image rights. Align each with local tax laws.
Plan bonuses & incentives efficiently	Structure performance bonuses linked to measurable achievements.
Leverage special tax regimes	Consider favourable tax regimes.

3. Image rights

Action item	Details
Establish a compliant image rights company	Assess the feasibility of using an IRC in a tax-efficient jurisdiction. Ensure the IRC has substance (physical office, staff, management).
Ensure proper contractual separation	Draft independent licensing agreements for image rights. Prevent reclassification as salary income.
Comply with transfer pricing & valuation rules	Ensure payments to the IRC align with arm's length principles. Conduct independent valuations to justify market rates.
Monitor anti-avoidance rules	Ensure the IRC meets economic substance requirements (staff, offices, management). Maintain records of licensing agreements.

4. Double taxation and relief mechanisms

Action item	Details
Identify applicable DTT provisions	Determine whether the exemption or credit method applies. Claim foreign tax credits to avoid double taxation.
Collect necessary documentation	Obtain tax residency certificates and proof of taxes paid abroad. Prepare supporting documents for DTT claims.
Plan for dual tax residency conflicts	Apply tie-breaker rules under relevant DTTs (permanent home, centre of vital interests, habitual abode, nationality).
File accurate tax returns	Ensure the player reports worldwide income in relevant jurisdictions. Claim foreign tax relief correctly to avoid penalties.

5. Tax indemnity and contract protection

Action item	Details
Include gross-up & indemnity clauses	Protect players from unexpected tax liabilities on salaries, signing-on fees, bonuses, and image rights income.
Address retroactive taxation risks	Specify which party bears reassessment risks. Include a club indemnity for payroll tax compliance errors.
Monitor regulatory & legal developments	Stay updated on tax law changes that impact contract structures. Conduct periodic contract reviews.

6. Post-transfer compliance and audits

Action item	Details
Monitor tax filing deadlines	Ensure all tax returns are filed on time in relevant jurisdictions. Work with local tax advisors.
Track residency status	Use travel logs and tax advisors to validate the player's primary tax residency.
Prepare for audits	Maintain detailed financial records for salary, bonuses, and endorsements.

Addendum: Tax Clauses Templates

This Addendum provides sample tax-related contract clauses developed from practical advisory experience across international football contracts. While each clause is jurisdiction-agnostic by design, legal validation should be sought in the relevant country of employment and residence.

a) Residency determination in the context of a loan agreement

The Player's tax residency shall be determined per the statutory residence rules of [Country of Employment] and the provisions of any applicable Double Tax Treaties. The responsibility for withholding and remitting taxes on the Player's income shall be allocated as follows:

- Parent Club (Parent Club Name): Responsible for fulfilling tax withholding obligations following the tax laws of (Parent Country).
- Loan Club (Loan Club Name): Responsible for fulfilling tax withholding obligations under the tax laws of (Loan Country). The Player agrees to submit accurate and appropriate documentation, including residency certificates, proof of physical presence, and any other documents required by relevant tax authorities.

b) Image Rights

1. Definitions

   - Image rights: The Player's name, image, likeness, signature, personal brand, and all associated intellectual property, as recognized under [applicable law].
   - IRC: The image rights Company [name of IRC] established by the player to hold and commercially exploit the Player's image rights, incorporated in [jurisdiction].

2. Grant of license

   - The Player, through the IRC, grants the Club a non-exclusive, limited-term license to use the Player's image rights strictly for commercial purposes, including but not limited to:
     - Merchandising.
     - Advertising campaigns.
     - Sponsorships, partnerships, and promotional materials.

   - The Club shall not use the Player's image rights in any manner that:
     - Violates applicable law.
     - Conflicts with pre-existing endorsements or sponsorship agreements held by the Player.

3. Compensation

   - The Club agrees to pay the IRC an annual fixed license fee of € [X], payable in [quarterly/monthly] instalments.
   - Any additional payments arising from Club-specific promotional campaigns or image rights activations shall be separately negotiated and agreed upon in writing.

- Fair market value (FMV): Payments to the IRC shall be aligned with market standards, supported by an independent valuation report to comply with transfer pricing regulations.

4. Tax compliance and regulatory obligations

   - The Club and the IRC acknowledge their obligation to comply with all applicable tax laws, including but not limited to:
     - Withholding obligations.
     - VAT/GST registration and reporting requirements.
     - Transfer pricing rules.
     - Payments to the IRC shall reflect the fair market value of the player's image rights, supported by independent valuation reports.

5. IRC substance and governance requirements

   - The IRC must:
     - Maintain operational substance in [Jurisdiction], including qualified personnel and a physical office.
     - Demonstrate active business activities, such as negotiating sponsorship agreements independently.
     - Provide an annual Certificate of Tax Residency, issued by the tax authorities in its jurisdiction.

If the IRC fails to meet substance requirements, the Club reserves the right to withhold payments pending compliance verification.

6. Tax indemnity and liability allocation

   - Player & IRC liability: The Player, through the IRC, shall indemnify the Club against any tax liabilities, penalties, or interest resulting from the IRC's non-compliance with tax laws.

- Club liability: The Club shall indemnify the Player and IRC against any penalties arising from:
    - Incorrect tax withholding or classification of payments made under this Clause.
    - Failure to comply with applicable local tax obligations affecting the Player's image rights income.

7. Term and Termination

- This image rights Agreement remains in effect for the duration of the Player's contract with the Club unless earlier terminated by mutual agreement.
- Upon termination:
    - The Club shall cease all use of the Player's image rights within [30] days.
    - Any outstanding payments due to the IRC shall be settled within [X] days of termination.
    - The Club may not use past promotional materials featuring the Player's image rights beyond the contract term, unless explicitly agreed upon.

c) Gross-up Agreement

This Gross-up agreement is made between:

- [Club name] ("the Club")
- [Player name] ("the Player")

This Agreement ensures that the Player receives a fixed net salary, with the Club assuming responsibility for all applicable tax liabilities, including income tax, social security contributions, and any other statutory deductions.

1. Definitions

Net salary: The agreed take-home salary the Player will receive after deducting all applicable taxes, levies, and contributions.

Gross-up amount: The Club must pay additional compensation to cover the applicable taxes and ensure the Player receives the full net salary.

Applicable tax rate: The combined tax burden, including:

- Income tax,
- Social security contributions (employer and employee),
- Any additional levies, surcharges, or solidarity contributions.

Tax-on-tax adjustment: Adjustments made to account for incremental tax liabilities arising from the grossing-up process.

Deferred payments: Any bonuses, severance payments, or other amounts due after the Player's termination or relocation to a different tax jurisdiction.

2. Club's obligation to Gross-up

2.1. Tax equalization guarantee:

If the Player is subject to income taxes on any portion of the salary (including, but not limited to, base salary, signing bonuses, or image rights payments) under the tax laws of [Country X], the Club shall ensure that the Player receives a fixed net amount of € [X] annually.

2.2. Scope of gross-up:

The Club agrees to pay an additional amount to ensure that the Player's net salary is fully preserved after deductions for:

- Income tax,
- Social security contributions,
- Applicable withholding taxes,
- Other mandatory levies, contributions or surcharges.

3. Tax-on-tax Adjustments

If the grossing-up of the Player's salary triggers additional tax liabilities (e.g., taxation of the gross-up amount itself), the Club agrees to adjust the gross-up amount iteratively until the Player receives the full net salary.

4. Post-Termination and Relocation Adjustments

The gross-up shall remain applicable to the following:

- Any deferred salary or signing bonuses.
- Performance-based bonuses are triggered after the contract ends.
- Termination or severance payments.

If the Player relocates to a jurisdiction with a higher tax rate, the Club will:

- Recalculate the gross-up amount based on the new jurisdiction's tax rate.
- Ensure the net deferred payments remain unaffected.

5. Adjustment for Tax Rate Increases

If the applicable tax rate increases during the contract period, the gross-up calculation shall be automatically adjusted to maintain the agreed net salary.

6. Risk Mitigation Provisions

The Club agrees to indemnify the Player against:

- Any penalties, fines, or back taxes arising from incorrect tax calculations.
- Any withholding tax disputes (unless caused by the Player's failure to provide correct information)."

d) Termination fee clause template

- "The Player is entitled to a termination payment equal to [amount or calculation method] as agreed upon in the termination settlement. The Club agrees to gross up the payment for any taxes arising in the Player's country of residence or the source jurisdiction, ensuring that the Player receives the full net amount specified herein. Furthermore, the Club shall indemnify the Player against any additional tax liabilities, penalties, or interest arising from this payment due to future audits, reclassification by tax authorities, or tax rate changes after the execution of this agreement."

e) Tax Indemnity Clause

1. Tax Indemnity Obligations

The Club agrees to indemnify and hold harmless the Player from and against any taxes, penalties, interest, or other liabilities (hereinafter referred to as "tax liabilities") imposed by any relevant tax authority arising from or related to the Player's income or benefits derived under this Agreement, including but not limited to:

- Salary and benefits in kind.
- Signing-on bonuses, loyalty bonuses, or other contractual payments.
- The Club pays agency commissions on behalf of the Player.

- Value-added tax (VAT) on benefits in kind.
- Penalties or interest due to late payments or misreporting by the Club.

The indemnity explicitly covers tax liabilities arising directly from:

- The Club's failure to withhold or remit taxes properly under applicable laws.
- Any misclassification of income by the Club.

2. Notification and cooperation

The Player agrees to notify the Club in writing within 30 days of receiving any communication from a tax authority that may result in tax liabilities covered under this clause. The Player shall provide all necessary documentation and cooperate fully with the Club to mitigate or dispute such tax liabilities, where feasible.

3. Termination and Survival

The obligations under this clause shall survive the termination of this Agreement for five (5) years or until the expiry of any applicable statute of limitations under relevant tax laws.

4. Reimbursement Terms

Reimbursement shall occur within 30 days of the Player providing evidence of tax liability. The Club retains the right to audit or contest claims before reimbursement.

f) Signing-on Fee Clause

1. Payment Terms

   - The Player shall receive a signing-on bonus of €[Amount], payable as follows:
     - 100% on July 15, 202X, upon the effective date of the transfer and commencement of employment with the Club.

   - The bonus is expressly linked to the Player's future employment with the Club, effective July 1, 202X, and does not constitute compensation for prior services.

2. Tax Obligations

   - The Player is responsible for complying with the tax laws of [Country A] and [Country B], including the timely declaration and payment of taxes related to the signing-on bonus.
   - The Club shall provide all necessary documentation, including payment records and proof of withholding, to assist the Player in meeting tax obligations.

3. Gross-up Provision

   - The Club agrees to gross up the signing-on bonus to ensure the Player receives a net amount of € [net amount] after taxes. The gross-up shall cover the national, regional, and local taxes in [Country A].

g) Liquidated Damages Clause

The (gross) amount to be paid resulting from the anticipated termination shall be paid considering the tax residence of the Player at the moment of the effective payment.

Printed in France by Amazon
Brétigny-sur-Orge, FR

32715407R00077